My Kaddish

A Child Speaks from the Warsaw Ghetto

Cherry
Orchard
Books

My Kaddish

A Child Speaks from the Warsaw Ghetto

Thérèse (Terri) Masson

Edited by Simone Masson

BOSTON

2024

Library of Congress Cataloging-in-Publication Data

Names: Masson, Th érèse C., 1937-2016, author. | Masson, Simone, 1974-editor.

Title: My kaddish: a child speaks from the Warsaw Ghetto / Th érèse (Terri) C. Masson, edited by Simone Masson.

Description: Boston: Cherry Orchard Books, 2023. | Includes bibliographical references.

Identifiers: LCCN 2024045800 (print) | LCCN 2024045801 (ebook) | ISBN 9798887192208 (hardback) | ISBN 9798887192215 (paperback) | ISBN 9798887192222 (adobe pdf) | ISBN 9798887192239 (epub)

Subjects: LCSH: Masson, Thérèse C., 1937-2016--Childhood and youth. | Masson, Thérèse C., 1937-2016--Family. | Getto warszawskie (Warsaw, Poland)--Biography. | Holocaust, Jewish (1939-1945)--Poland--Personal narratives. | Holocaust survivors--United States--Califronia--Biography. | Jewish children in the Holocaust--Poland--Biography. | Jewish children in the Holocaust--Poland--Warsaw. | Golub-Dobrzyń (Poland) v Biography.

Classification: LCC DS134.72.M3794 A3 2024 (print) | LCC DS134.72.M3794 (ebook) | DDC 940.53/18092 [B]--dc23/eng/20240928

LC record available at https://lccn.loc.gov/2024045800
LC ebook record available at https://lccn.loc.gov/2024045801
Copyright © 2024, Academic Studies Press
All rights reserved.

ISBN 9798887192208 (hardback)
ISBN 9798887192215 (paperback)
ISBN 9798887192222 (adobe pdf)
ISBN 9798887192239 (epub)

Book design by PHi Business Solutions
Cover design by Ivan Grave

Published by Cherry Orchard Books, an imprint of
Academic Studies Press
1577 Beacon Street
Brookline, MA 02446, USA
press@academicstudiespress.com
www.academicstudiespress.com

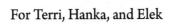

For Terri, Hanka, and Elek

Contents

Foreword

It is 2016 and my mom, Thérèse (Terri) Masson, born Klara Alter, has died. She died on February 15, after suffering a debilitating stroke seven months before. I am heartbroken. My mom was a truly remarkable human being—full of love, life, generosity, and wild optimism. She had a brilliant mind and an enormous heart. Like her mother, my beloved grandmother, she was a survivor. As a young child she survived, as she put it, "The war of all wars [. . .] a persecution that gave rise to the term genocide." She survived, not psychically intact, in fact deeply wounded, but whole enough to become the mother that I knew—a vivacious person, tirelessly carrying on a legacy of love.

My mom was both incredibly constricted by her past and unfathomably free. I cannot explain how this worked. But to know my mom was to know someone who lived seemingly without constraints. She was full of joy and quick to forgive; she didn't care about petty matters and she didn't mind being inconvenienced. She almost always saw the bigger picture, and she could get to the deep truth, the heart of any matter, in an instant, while others languished on the periphery.

With that said, to read this memoir, is to understand my mom as someone who suffered deeply for her entire life from the traumas she suffered as a child. Haunted by nightmares and painful memories, plagued by compulsions and uncontrollable, self-destructive tendencies, she was burdened by a "cavernous sorrow [... that] will continue with me, inhabiting the edge of my consciousness to the end of my days." My mom suffered greatly.

So how to reconcile these two parallel truths? I don't know. My mom is no longer here to ask. She would surely have an answer. What we have is her memoir. Short as it is, unfinished, with a list in capitalized letters on the last page of all that she still wanted to recount, it contains her words, tells her story, and commits to paper the experiences that she carried inside her until the end of her life. And not only does she tell the story of her family's survival as she remembers it, she manages to engage in a kind of self-analysis through which she discovers how these terrible events shaped her character. I am grateful to her for this—for having the courage to tell the story, for these invaluable gifts of memory and insight.

In the pages that follow, my mom tells the story of her survival as a Jewish child in the Warsaw Ghetto, in hiding on the Aryan side, and fleeing east with her mother and father to meet the oncoming Red Army. Two years old at the outbreak of the war, she was eight by the end, so the memories are fragmented, incomplete, but nevertheless vivid and evocative. Interspersed with memories of wartime are reflections from the present and occasional tidbits from her adult life. But the narrative ends abruptly. I know that my mom intended to write more, but after completing a revision in 2008, she did not continue writing.

In order to give some sense of what happened after the manuscript ends, I have included an epilogue comprised of excerpts from a brief biographical timeline she wrote in 2005, around the same time she began working on this memoir. Additionally, with the help of my father, someone with a deep knowledge of the Holocaust, I have included a timeline of historical events, as well as a glossary of selected terms used in the text. Finally, there is a collection of family photographs, annotated with names and approximate dates. Without being able to consult my mom or grandmother for more precise details, it is the best I could do.

My mom began writing her memoir in 2005 at age sixty-seven following a trip to Warsaw that she and I took together, her first time back to Poland since leaving as a child in 1946. As she remarks, "now at last as an old woman, I am driven to do so [write]." This would be the first of four trips to Warsaw that she and I took together—harrowing journeys, yet deeply rewarding. We went first in 2004, and then returned in 2005, 2006, and finally in 2014 for the opening of the Museum of the History of Polish Jews.

On our first trip, we met family we did not know we had, who still lived in Warsaw. And we met a remarkable woman, Elżbieta Janicka, who would become a dear friend, and who broke through the icy Polish silence, the emptiness, the disregard, to help us find some connection to our past, some fragment of hope and truth in the sea of loss that was tossing us about. Over the course of the next two trips, we found the home my mom refers to at the beginning of her story as her family's summer house in Kutno. Sixty years after the events in her memoir, the house was shockingly distinct—just like the image in the photograph. We also obtained my mom's birth certificate, which, despite being fake and issued after the war, felt like a small triumph.

We spent time with our long-lost family and new friend and many hours walking the streets of Warsaw with maps of the ghetto in our hands and my mom's memories coming to her in flashes—a street name, a number, an image. We spent two mournful afternoons among the stones at Treblinka, and twice we visited the site of the *Umschlagplatz*.[1] These were indescribably difficult and sad occasions.

On our last trip, my mom insisted on going to the opening of the Jewish Museum. Just before the opening night we crossed paths with a young man who worked there. When we explained that my mom had returned to Warsaw for this event at the museum, and that she had survived the Warsaw Ghetto as a child, he told us that we could not attend the reception. The museum could not, he added, be expected to extend invitations to "all the survivors."

My mom writes many times in her memoir that she wishes she had talked more and shared more with her mother and father, that she felt their pain imprinted on her and would have liked to tell them. But my mom was not able to face the pain until her later years, when her parents were already long gone. She writes of her mother: "But through her whole life after these sad times, I could not tell her how I remembered and I could never mourn with her. My failure in this, I so deeply regret."

Now that my mom is also gone, I feel this longing arising in me, a regret, a sense that I did not adequately convey to her the ways that her story, my family's story, lives on inside me. I carry the lament differently. I did not experience these events directly, of course, and time, the passing of generations,

---

1   *Umschlagplatz* was the railway yard where Warsaw's Jews were concentrated and then loaded onto cattle trucks going to Treblinka.

weaves these ancestral threads in different ways for each generation. And I do carry the threads, woven around my heart. What happened to my mom, her parents, grandparents, aunts, uncles, cousins, and friends is also a part of me.

My mother writes: "I wish I could excise it onto a dark canvas that would continue to bear witness when I am gone to dust." Though she never did paint, in these pages she has her canvas, one that allows me, and her new readers, to continue to bear witness now that her memory alone remains. Thank you, Mom, for your enduring love, for living so freely, for your bravery in creating this canvas. May we never forget.

Simone Masson
Oakland, California
May, 2016

Preface

The twentieth century has become known as the era of the witness. Millions of people witnessed in broad daylight the persecution of Jews in Europe and North Africa. Thousands of people, Germans and non-Germans alike, took part in the subsequent genocide resulting in the murder of six million Jewish men, women, and children. Since then, over a period of more than eighty years, more than one hundred thousand Holocaust testimonies have been collected. No other event in history has left behind such a magnitude of eyewitness accounts. Jewish voices constitute the most important body of egodocuments (*ego* is the Latin word for *I*) pertaining to the history of the Holocaust and to the transmission of individual and collective memory. Within the vast, ever-increasing Holocaust literature, Thérèse C. Masson's childhood memoir stands out. *My Kaddish* is a compelling, intriguing testimony.

Let me set the scene by briefly contextualizing and outlining the distinct features of this memoir. Thérèse's recollections are not designed as a historical narrative. Intertwining history and memory, they present and connect early childhood images and episodes with postwar events, reflections, and, above all, the traumatic experiences which shaped her character and life.

Testimonies of Holocaust survivors fulfil many functions. First and foremost, they are responses to Nazi persecution, offering a window into the destruction of Jewish life and recording the experience of suffering and devastation, resilience and survival. They also create, in Elie Wiesel's words, "invisible tombstones, erected to the memory of the unburied." Murdered Jews were denied resting places in Jewish cemeteries—indeed, in any cemeteries. *My Kaddish* is Thérèse C. Masson's prayer of mourning for her murdered family and the Jewish world that has been destroyed. She restores family ties—a cornerstone of Jewish culture.

Her daughter, Simone, a health professional specializing in the diagnosis of people with dementia and Alzheimer's disease, assisted in writing and editing the memoir. Her ex-husband and close friend, Jeffrey Moussaieff Masson, a renowned academic and prolific writer, also provided assistance. They inserted a historical timeline and a glossary. They produced a fascinating portrayal of Thérèse and collected a set of photos, which document an intimate circle of family and friends.

Witnesses to the horror of the Holocaust recorded their experiences in successive phases. The first phase in the evolution of the role and image of the Holocaust witness dates back to the war years, to the unfolding "Jewish Catastrophe" or *Churbn*, the Yiddish term common at the time for the destruction of European Jewry. Incarcerated in ghettos and camps or escaping into the underground, Jews wrote down their experiences in pamphlets, diaries, or notebooks, in letters or post cards. Many were murdered; only fragments of their writings have been unearthed.

With their liberation, the second phase began. Wherever survivors were registered—in displaced persons camps (DP camps) or refugee shelters, in Jewish communities or relief organizations—they were asked to tell their stories. Names and places contained in early questionnaires and protocols aided in the search for missing relatives and friends, a search which continues to this very day. Descendants of survivors relied on these data when tracing their family history.

Like so many testimonies, *My Kaddish* is a "lighthouse" that provides guidance for Holocaust research, education, and remembrance. It fulfils Emil Fackenheim's "614th Commandment"—the obligation to keep the memory of the Holocaust alive. Obliged to remember, the witness, writer, and reader pass on the knowledge and experience of the Holocaust to subsequent generations; and in doing so, they ensure the continuity of Jewish life and deny Adolf Hitler and the executioners of the Final Solution a posthumous victory.

Some thirty thousand testimonies were collected in the immediate postwar period, at a time when memories were still fresh. They challenge the enduring myth of the postwar silence of Holocaust survivors. They graphically reveal the brutality and terror survivors encountered. In their immediacy and rawness, they often give way to aggression and anguish at the recent suffering and loss. They are profoundly different and more significant for the history of the Holocaust than later recollections, which, with the passage of time, are more relevant for studies of the Holocaust's aftermath, as they shed light on the postwar life of survivors.

The third phase commenced when survivors testified in Nazi war crimes trials. Statements and affidavits given to the police and in court rooms played a vital role in tracing and bringing perpetrators to justice. The Eichmann trial in Jerusalem (1961) signaled the emergence of the Holocaust witness as "bearer of history."

The fourth phase began a few years later, with the end of the Cold War and the opening of secret archives in Eastern Europe, which triggered an explosion of Holocaust research and projects. Many survivors and their descendants began to tell their stories, and there was a massive wave of testimonies, recorded by "oral history" programs or in Steven Spielberg's monumental audiovisual project, which captured more than fifty-two thousand voices and faces.[1] These testimonies paved the way for what has been termed "memory work." *My Kaddish* is among such testimonies, as it illustrates how memory works. This phase has made one thing clear: soon there will be no living witnesses to the horror of the Holocaust. The accounts we have are preserved in their original forms in archival depositories across the globe or in publications. A few will be transformed by modern technology and made visually accessible by virtual reconstruction. Child survivors, now at an advanced age, are the last living witnesses of the Holocaust. Thérèse herself wrote her childhood memoirs in the last years of her life.

Born in 1937 in the Polish city of Golub-Dobrzyn, Thérèse Masson, nee Klara Alter, spent her early childhood years behind the walls of the Warsaw Ghetto and in the underground on the "Aryan side," first hidden in a bunker, then in an abandoned farmhouse located in the forest. In 1946, she left Poland with her parents, and embarked on a long journey with stopovers in France, England, and Canada, finally settling down in California. She commenced her professional career

---

1   See "Film and Video Archive," United States Holocaust Museum, accessed 1 August 2023, https://www.ushmm.org/collections/the-museums-collections/about/film-and-video-archive.

as a translator and high school history teacher. Later, she made her mark as a writer, presenter, and producer in the worlds of radio, TV, and theatre. As a mature student, she obtained a law degree and practiced as a lawyer and legal consultant. In addition, she was deeply attracted to philosophy and psychoanalysis. Like most survivors, she was haunted by nightmares and painful memories of the terror and trauma she experienced as a child. While two of her marriages ended in divorce, she spent the last thirty-seven years with her partner, Deborah, and daughter, Simone.

It was half a century before Thérèse's silence was broken. Two events provided the decisive impulses. In 2002, Thérèse suffered a brain aneurism that required surgery. The recovery reignited her feeling of being a survivor. In 2004, she travelled to Poland, visiting places from her early childhood which she only vaguely remembered. Upon her return in 2005, and at the age of sixty-seven, she began writing her memoir. The *Spurensuche*, the search for traces of her lost family and early childhood, continued until 2014. The trips to Poland refreshed her memory. Furthermore, relatives were located and new friends made. Thérèse visited a villa in the countryside which, before the war, had been the family's summer house. She walked to locations that were once in the Warsaw Ghetto, looking for the building and backyard which had once confined her. She went to the Umschlagplatz, the collecting point from which the ghetto's inmates were deported to the Treblinka extermination camp. She found her way to Powazki Street and the cemetery where she had spent some time as a child. She returned to where the bunker that was her first hideout after escaping from the ghetto.

My Kaddish depicts the landscapes of her early childhood, transforming them into memorial sites. Visual images and sensory triggers link the past and present: buildings and rooms, walls and backyards, streets and squares, gardens and trees; smells and sounds, light and darkness, warmth and cold, fear and joy, pain and loneliness. These early memories determine the remembrance of events and sentiments. However, they are constantly interrupted by and enmeshed with contemporary episodes and reflections. What finally emerges is a striking self-analysis which not only illustrates how this childhood memoir has been constructed but also reveals the psychological burdens and damage of a child survivor. *My Kaddish* is an important and challenging autobiographical account of the trauma, the wounds, Thérèse experienced as a child during the Holocaust—wounds which never healed and that shaped her postwar life.

Emeritus Professor Dr. Konrad Kwiet
Resident historian, Sydney Jewish Museum
2018

Historical Timeline

January 30, 1933. The Nazi party takes power in Germany. Hitler is elected chancellor.

March 22, 1933. The first Nazi concentration camp is established at Dachau. The initial prisoners are political opponents.

April 7, 1933. The Law for the Restoration of the Professional Civil Service bars Jews from holding positions in the civil service, at universities, and government.

May 10, 1933. Books by Jews and opponents of Nazism are publicly burned.

July 14, 1933. Legislation is adopted that allows for the forced sterilization of Roma and Sinti people, people with disabilities, African Germans, and others considered "inferior to the Aryan race."

September 15, 1935. The anti-Jewish "Nuremberg Laws" are enacted. Jews are no longer considered German citizens, cannot marry Aryans, and are banned from flying the German flag.

March 3, 1936. Jewish doctors are barred from practicing medicine.

July 6, 1938. Representatives from thirty-two countries meet at Evian, France, to discuss refugee policies. Most of the countries refuse to let in more Jewish refugees.

August 17, 1938. Jewish men are forced to take the middle name Israel; Jewish women, the middle name Sarah.

November 9, 1938. Kristallnacht: a nationwide attack on the Jewish population of Germany, including the burning of synagogues, looting of Jewish homes, businesses, and cemeteries, and the murder of Jewish people.

November 12, 1938. All Jewish businesses in Germany closed by decree.

January 30, 1939. In a Reichstag speech, Hitler states that if war erupts, "the result will be not the Bolshevization of earth, and thus a Jewish victory, but the annihilation of the Jewish race in Europe."

September 1, 1939. Hitler invades Poland.

September 3, 1939. England and France declare war on Germany: World War II has begun.

October, 1939. With Aktion T4, the so-called "euthanasia program," Hitler extends powers to doctors (especially psychiatrists) to kill institutionalized mentally and physically disabled people.

October, 1939. The first Polish ghetto is established in Piotrków.

December, 1939. All Jewish males in Poland between the ages of fourteen and sixty are conscripted for forced labor.

May 20, 1940. The Auschwitz concentration camp is established.

November 15, 1940. The Warsaw Ghetto, containing nearly five hundred thousand Jews, is sealed off.

February 1, 1941. The German authorities begin rounding up Polish Jews for transfer to the Warsaw Ghetto. Ten thousand Jews die from starvation in the ghetto between January and June 1941. An estimated ninety-two thousand people die from starvation in the ghetto before the 1942 mass deportation (Grossaktion Warschau) begins.

March 3, 1941. The Kraków Ghetto is established, with fifteen to twenty thousand Jewish people living within its boundaries.

June 22, 1941. Nazi Germany invades the USSR (Operation Barbarossa): massacres of Jewish women, children, and men are perpetrated by the Einsatzgruppen and local populations (Odessa, Jedwabne, etc.)

September 1, 1941. All Jews above the age of six in Germany and German territories are forced to wear a Star of David sewed on the left side of their clothes with the word *Jude* printed in black.

October 15, 1941. Jews from Germany, Austria, and Czechoslovakia are deported to Poland.

October 15, 1941. Operation Reinhard begins, which was ultimately responsible for the murder of approximately 1.7 million Jews, most of them Polish. The majority of victims were Jews deported from ghettos in Poland to the killing centers of Bełżec, Sobibór, and Treblinka.

December 8, 1941. The Chełmno death camp opens near Lódz, in occupied Poland, and the first gassing of victims with poison gas occurs.

December 8, 1941. The United States declares war on Japan.

December 16, 1941. During a cabinet meeting, Hans Frank, gauleiter of Poland, states: "Gentlemen, I must ask you to rid yourselves of all feeling of pity. We must annihilate the Jews wherever we find them and wherever it is possible in order to maintain there the structure of the Reich as a whole."

December 1941–January 1942. Five thousand Austrian Roma and Sinti people from the Łódź ghetto are deported to the killing center at Chełmno, where they are gassed in mobile vans.

1942. The mass murder of Jews in gas chambers begins in Nazi extermination camps located in occupied Poland at Auschwitz, Birkenau, Treblinka, Sobibór, Bełżec, and Majdanek-Lublin.

January 16, 1942. More than sixty-five thousand Jews in the Łódź ghetto are deported to the killing center at Chełmno and gassed to death.

January 20, 1942. The Wannsee Conference in Berlin: Heydrich outlines the plan to murder Europe's Jews, some eleven million people.

March 1, 1942. The establishment of Auschwitz-Birkenau for the extermination of Jews, Roma, and Sinti; Poles, Soviet POWs, and others are also murdered at the camp.

July 23–September 12, 1942. Mass deportations of Jews from the Warsaw Ghetto to the new killing center, Treblinka. After the deportations, only sixty thousand Jews remain.

July 23, 1942. Adam Czerniaków, head of the Judenrat, commits suicide rather than turn over Jewish children to the Germans. Standing in solidarity with the children and all the other ghetto inmates, he refused to sign the German announcement of the deportation of Warsaw Jews. The announcement was displayed on the walls without his signature.

July 28, 1942. Jewish fighting organizations are organized in the Warsaw Ghetto.

January 18, 1943. The second wave of deportations. Organized resistance by Jews in the ghetto commences.

April 19, 1943. The German forces plan to liquidate the Warsaw Ghetto on the eve of Passover. During the Warsaw Ghetto Uprising, the Jewish resistance fights the Germans for almost a month.

May 16, 1943. The liquidation of the Warsaw Ghetto. SS and Police Chief Jurgen Stroop proclaims: "180 Jews, bandits, and subhumans were destroyed. The Jewish quarter of Warsaw is no more." Stroop personally pushes the detonator button to demolish the Great Synagogue of Warsaw. He later recalls: "What a marvelous sight it was. A fantastic piece of theater [. . .]. I glanced over at my brave officers and men, tired and dirty, silhouetted against the glow of the burning buildings. After prolonging the suspense for a moment, I shouted Heil Hitler and pressed the button" (Jürgen Stroop, *Conversations with an Executioner*).

June 6, 1944. D-Day: Allied landing at Normandy.

August 1, 1944. The Warsaw Uprising begins.

November 25, 1944. The Nazis order the destruction of crematoria and gas chambers. All traces of their crimes are to disappear.

January 17, 1945. The Nazis empty Auschwitz and start prisoners on "death marches" to Germany and the Bergen-Belsen concentration camp.

January 27, 1945. Soviet troops liberate the Auschwitz camp complex.

April 30, 1945. Adolf Hitler commits suicide.

May 7, 1945. Germany surrenders; the end of the Third Reich; the war in Europe is over.

November, 1945. War crimes tribunal convened in Nuremberg, Germany.

July 4, 1946. A massacre of Jews in the Polish town of Kielce. This occurs in the context of considerable anti-Jewish violence in postwar Poland. Many Polish Jews come to believe that there is no future for Jews in in the country.

CHAPTER 1

The Beginning

———————

This is the brief chronology of my life that I have been intending to produce for so long . . .

. . .

I was born in Golub or Rypin, in Poland, on my grandfather's estate on June 13, 1937. I think my mother's water broke a little early (which is also how Simone, my daughter, announced her arrival). The intention had been to take my mother to the hospital in Dobrzyn, the closest city, but there was no time, so my father, a physician, delivered me right then and there.

Prewar, I remember the feel of my nanny, her softness, and of my father's younger brother, Badza, because he threw me up in the air. These memories are mainly of a feeling and almost a texture.

My first actual visual memory is of big, shiny black boots that I feared, and the effort of throwing dirt or sand onto those boots. I do not remember seeing any of it land and mar that shiny surface, but I know that that is what I tried to achieve. Even now, I see them at eye level and the image makes me fearful. I was later told that a high-ranking German officer, who somehow knew my, mother came to visit her to tell her that the war was coming and that she should leave Poland immediately. Apparently, my mother and this officer had a long and animated discussion in German. My mother had studied in Berlin in the late '20s before she went to the university in Liège, where she met my father, then a medical student; she was linguistically talented and spoke a beautiful "high" German. All this occurred in my family's home in Kutno, about seventy-five kilometers from Warsaw, where they had a villa—a summer house in a garden—that they evidently visited just before the outbreak of war. I had just turned two years old when these events occurred; it was late summer 1939.

I also have an auditory memory from this period. The sound of gunfire, bombs, and explosions when the war broke out in September 1939 and the front approached. All of these memories are wrapped in a profound sadness, a feeling of being lost, left alone and bereft. This may be because I lost my beloved nanny at this time. Janka was a young Polish woman, a Christian, probably a devout Catholic, and my parents sent her away out of fear and suspicion.

The sadness that descends upon me when I try to grapple with these thoughts and unravel these feelings is pervasive and almost paralyzing, making it difficult for me to write; yet, at the same time, now at last as an old woman, I am driven to do so. I am a prolific writer, and once I begin, the words flow. It is the beginning that is so difficult. I wonder if this fear and near paralysis of mind that overwhelms me whenever I come face-to-face with that blank piece of paper, actual or virtual, is an echo of the profound and paralyzing dread that I have of my own memory, suppressed for so long, perhaps, bubbling up, too close to the surface, when I face that blank page. Who knows what terrible images of evil and horror that I fought so hard and paid such a heavy price my whole life to push down, to deny and to avoid, might break the surface onto that blank page, now that my guard is down.

CHAPTER 2

The Warsaw Ghetto

1940 and 1941 in the Warsaw Ghetto. I was three and four years old. I remember steel-gray hair, prominent cheek bones, dark eyes, a sad beautiful face, scratchy clothes. That was my grandmother, my mother's mother; it was a dark space, with rough boards and dirt on the floor. I suppose, now, that it was my grandparents' hiding place, where we all lived together. Old people and children did not have work cards for slave labor in the factories; they had to stay in hiding all the time and would immediately be brutally murdered if found. This hiding place was below the floorboards of a building because I remember being shushed to keep absolutely still; I remember the feeling of being transfixed with fear and hearing boots and banging above, sometimes screams of pain and fear.

There was a formidable iron stove somewhere there because I remember the rough rusty look of it, and I know that my grandmother made me French toast from very old bread pieces soaked in diluted ersatz (synthetic, imitation) coffee. I remember the look of almost charred bits and pieces and the bitter taste that I still love. It was a great delicacy for an occasion when I had French toast. I do not remember the occasions, maybe Passover, because I have the word stuck in my mind as *Pesach*, and for some reason I love that word and associate it with that taste.

All I remember of my grandfather at that time is someone very big who had to squeeze and stoop to come in through the opening. But I do remember him later, vividly, at the Umschhlagplatz.

The other visual memory I have in my mind's eye of the Ghetto is a cobblestone street with bodies of people partly covered by torn newspaper. The faces of the bodies looking as gray as the stones with huge flies buzzing. I also remember the look of the wall surrounding the Ghetto. It seemed tall, up to the sky, to me, thick and totally impenetrable, with rusty barbed wire on top.

It happened one day, by the wall, when the light was dark, either because it was a stormy overcast day or because it was almost night, that my mother gave me a Kaiser roll with sliced radishes inside. I know I took one bite because I remember the taste of the radish, which I still love, when a little boy urchin at a run grabbed the bun *en passant*. I wailed to get back my bun. And this is the first lesson in life that I remember from my mother, who refused to try to get the bun back from the boy and told me that he needed it more than I because he was an urchin who did not have a mama or anyone to care for him.

This is also my first memory of the feeling of hunger. I remember that feeling of a painful void in my stomach demanding to be filled that I re-experience frequently in my life when I sit to eat something I love. I eat so quickly and so much that the fullness is sometimes painful, always very uncomfortable. Yet I cannot stop. And occasionally I relive this experience, thus, to this day.

. . .

I know that I have other images, sounds, and feelings in my mind from this time—but the Umschlagplatz experience is so overwhelming in my mind that I really have to address that before I continue with prior, or what I now believe are prior, memories. Perhaps this is because that is the experience that I relived in an awful paranoid episode I suffered in the hospital for a few days, after the brain trauma of a bleed, surgery, and subsequent air embolism. I should explain how it is that now, sixty years after these terrible events, that I am trying to memorialize and describe here, I became a survivor again, trapped in desperate fear.

It was unfortunately late in life, long after I was past doing physical things really well, that I discovered a love and a need for the invigoration of regular exercise and the exhilaration of running. I became totally addicted to my regular morning routine of dancing exercise followed by jogging around my very hilly neighborhood. On this particular morning in late March 2002, I felt tired and didn't feel like going out, especially as it was cold and overcast. But, compulsive maniac that I was, intent on these obsessive activities, in retrospect, all in the vain and unsuccessful service of the work of denial and the endless and very hard labor of trying to suppress the irrepressible thrust of thoughts, feelings, and images that were not successfully eliminated even after a lifetime of trying to ban them forever, I forced myself to go out to run.

I am not sure when, but I think on the last leg of the jog, I suddenly had the worst pain in my head I had ever experienced or could imagine. It was well beyond a headache. Then I felt very dizzy. I was in front of a picture window and by a telephone post. The last thing I remember is trying to lean on that post. The people in the house beyond the picture window called 911. By the time the ambulance arrived, I had come to and was talking. I told them who I was and who to call. I even gave them the phone number. I remember nothing of this and nothing much of the next three months in the hospital, except for the experience of the paranoid episode in which I was lost for three or four days, trapped inside the terror and images of the Umschlagplatz.

What occurred was that I suffered a brain aneurysm with a major bleed. In the hospital, a surgeon, in a six-hour brain surgery, successfully clipped the aneurysm. I survived. After the operation, I began the recovery. Then, one night, inexplicably, I pulled out the central lines from my jugular veins, leaving the ports open to the air. I suffered an air embolism to the brain. I was unconscious and unresponsive for three days. Again, I survived. It took three years, but I have worked my way back to mental and physical mobility. I still have some serious deficits, but I have not given up yet.

I know that one of the huge personality problems my childhood created in me is an inability to save or to plan for tomorrow. This is because, of course, on the one hand, I do not know for sure that there will be a tomorrow, but, on the other hand, I do know that I am indestructible, so precautions and other such safety maneuvers are unnecessary. Que será, será, and I will be there.

CHAPTER 3

Umschlagplatz

As everyone now knows, the Umschlagplatz in the Warsaw Ghetto was the most extraordinary event of the entire period. The German high command decided to complete the Final Solution in Warsaw, but still the Protestant ethic of economy, never waste anything, prevailed. So, unlike other conquerors, these good Protestant Germans did not sack the Ghetto, murder everyone left, and then burn it to the ground. They proceeded systematically to squeeze out and obtain anything possible from what was left after so much murder, torture, starvation, and typhus, before they sacked it and then burned it to the ground.

First came the order: everyone must march to the Umschlagplatz under penalty of death if found remaining. What I remember of the march is almost unbearable discomfort, a deep feeling of dread and being very hot. I was hidden under my mother's coat and under strict instructions to remain absolutely quiet and invisible. Small children were totally useless, therefore totally expendable, even more at risk than old people.

I remember the scene with the selection table in the middle. That is what I saw in such extraordinary detail in my mind's eye, where I was trapped, in the hospital. If only I could draw.

I was trapped inside an overwhelming fear, and all I heard were sad wails here and there. In my mind, but for these mournful and eerie sounds, there is a weird silence as I see my grandfather standing tall in front of the table, his face carved in stone, his chin up as if he were looking beyond. My grandmother stands next to him, looking much smaller. Then, a sudden, very loud burst of gunfire, and my grandmother drops. I must have moved up on my mother's body to see because my perspective is higher. My grandfather picks her up, her head lolls, and I feel my mother scream and wail. Then, as a soldier began to hit my grandfather with the butt of his rifle to move him away from the table and into the thick column of people moving slowly, I now know, to the trains to Treblinka, my mother's whole body twisted and screamed out with a pain that I felt with every cell of my body. That memory of my mother's pain is so deeply ingrained in every part of me that I know it to be truly a somatic memory, forever imprinted in me.

My mother always said that the worst moment of the war to her was the choice between trying to save me or running to the aid of her beloved parents. I know this was that tortured moment for her that she could never put aside or escape from. At that moment when her entire body screamed in despair, I felt the scream. But through the rest of her life after these sad times, I could not tell her how I remembered and I could never mourn with her. My failure in this, I so deeply regret. I know, in some way, every day of my life, this fathomless, cavernous sorrow haunts me and will continue with me, inhabiting the edge of my consciousness to the end of my days.

I have a dream that, though I don't remember all the different occasions, I know I have dreamt many times. I know the dream stems from this event, from this memory, and the terrible isolation from my mother that I required later in life to survive, to remove myself from the inferno of her suffering and of my mind's eye. The bare outline of this dream that I associate with this memory is: I feel a terrible terror; I know I am trying to get away from mad, murderous pursuers, and I am trying to scream for help, but I am totally encased in glass that surrounds me and wraps me like plastic; so I cannot move and my screams cannot be heard, cannot even emerge.

. . .

This dream was actually quite elaborate and detailed. Sometimes I remember more; but not today. Like my memories of actual events, images, textures, sounds and feelings, my memories of these tortured dreams come and go, set off by random events in my daily life. The other day, for example, there was a very large black fly in the bathroom with me, and there in my mind was the scene of corpses on the cobblestone street in the Ghetto, as clear as day. I could see them in every detail from close by because as a small child I would have been much closer to them than a tall adult, and that was the perspective from which I viewed this image in my mind. Sometimes this is quite off-putting or disturbing, but most of the time I am able to defend myself from it right away.

Mostly I have learnt how to avoid any surge of feelings by simply and strongly focusing on something as different as possible and becoming totally insistent, absorbed, and obsessive about the secondary, distracting line of thought or observation. These are, perhaps, the mechanics, the very means of denial. And if they don't work, beware! Perhaps that's what happened to me in the hospital. I say this because it was there that I saw the Umschlagplatz selection table in such extraordinary detail, including papers, pistols, and faces—in full face and profile that, if I could paint, would be a dark but populated canvas like those scenes from the middle ages in which the deep darkness is filled with the terrible terror that enveloped me in the hospital, out from which I could not emerge, until suddenly it was gone, dropped away from me like an unwanted cloak or skin. The occasion: a pleasant conversation with someone I liked, the hospital neuropsychologist. Perhaps she just did not fit the memory. I don't know, still. And I also do not know, still, if what I remembered with such photographic intensity was the actual image preserved in my mind, as Freud said, like an archaeological layer, complete in all its detail, needing only to be correctly reconstructed; or the memory of a later dream, or a strange creation of my paranoid state. The fact is, though, these were real people around that table. Who were they and from what part of my life, in actuality, did they emerge? And does that matter after all? Are false memories of traumas that actually occurred, false? And what of any importance do they actually misrepresent?

. . .

I am thinking here of superb literary creations like Jerzy Kosiński's *The Painted Bird*; of course, he was not a good or a nice man. He was not a mensch. I spoke with him—I know: he was narcissistic and very bizarre. What sane young mensch that you know would make up that past as the chosen fantasy of his own origins? But, what he wrote, though false, as his own past, was uncannily accurate as a description of what occurred in Poland in those sad and bizarre times.

I remember, but again only in general outline today, another dream that I know is related to these events. This dream is chameleon-like, like my means of survival itself. So it can only be described in outline. But I know that, although I have not actually dreamt it for a long time, sometimes I remember details of some of its incarnations. The dream is that I am being pursued or attacked somewhere enclosed. But I am not alone. I must save someone else whom I love. I devise a means of escape or, more satisfying in the dream, I fight the attackers and I prevail. This happened more often in this dream, in the period when, as a young adult, I trained in martial arts. The problem with this dream was that many, many times, I could not find a means of survival and would then force myself back into the dream to try and try again. Eventually, I would have to get up, sometimes manic with a sense of mastery, but more often exhausted, depleted, wrung out emotionally.

Of course, our war went on for many years, nearly six years for us, of German occupation, so it is very hard to know just what event or period caused what dream or set of feelings, trait of character, or mindset.

So, just to carry on chronologically as much as I can, after the Umschlagplatz, life in the Ghetto was really at an end: so many were dead of starvation or typhus or both; most of the rest were deported to burn in Treblinka, and those few remaining with any health and energy were planning a bloody fighting end, the Ghetto Uprising. My father, even then, was a pacifist. Oddly, I do not remember the word in Polish, but I know he explained to me what it meant, saying that it meant that he could not, would not fight physically; he would not injure anyone. He said that, above all, he was a doctor and he had taken an oath to heal, not to kill. To resist and disobey was the right human response; the ability to rebel was a wonderful human quality; but to wreak destruction and hurt others was a great wrong. He was still tending to the sick every day, had a make-shift hospital, and for that reason he refused to leave until the very last moment (who would care for his patients if he was gone?). My mother, again, was preoccupied with how to save me, make my father leave, and how to escape to the Warsaw beyond the wall, the Aryan side, where life still went on.

After the Umschlagplatz, I have a pervasive visual feeling of emptiness, in the sense of no people around in what had been, before, crowded streets and places. It was about this time, too, that I remember my father started giving me powder he scraped from sidewalks or unpainted walls to eat for calcium, a practice he continued until after the war. I presume that is why I grew straight without deformities despite some prolonged bouts of starvation.

After the war, I remember vomiting after my first drink of milk, an aversion I have retained to this day. I only like milk if the fat is removed and the milk is mixed with something bit-ter like strong coffee. For a long time after the war, my father insisted that I drink carrot juice and eat mostly carrots, rad-ishes, sweet peas, and spinach. I know I must have eaten other foods, but that is mostly what I remember of my postwar diet in Poland.

It was during this period in the Ghetto in late 1942, after the Umschlagplatz, that I became very ill. Everything in my throat hurt and swelled so that I could not breathe. My father later told me that I had diphtheria because of the corpses and the rats. He told me he had to get a special serum to make me bet-ter. One day, he came rushing in and gave me something very bitter that I liked. I must have recovered very quickly because

I do not remember being sick anymore except that, a little later, I developed a big visible lump in my throat, a goiter. My father gave me iodine spread on everything I ate: little pieces of crumbly bread, the occasional delicacy of a cooked potato, onion, a radish or a carrot.

...

It seems odd to me that I do not remember more from the Umschlagplatz events because that was Yom Kippur 1942 and I was five, old enough so I should remember. I know these images are there, deep in me, and one day, perhaps when my day of judgment comes, I will retrieve them and then be able to truly mourn.

...

I know that there was an earlier time in 1941 in the Ghetto. I was four when my father, sick and broken, held me close and explained to me the evils of war. He loved to draw for me and he drew me a picture of pacifism. It was a whole line of people, smiling, jumping, dancing, and holding hands. My father's drawings were childlike, primitive, and always illustrative. At the end of his life he became a painter, finally, producing small, primitive, canvasses, so detailed that he often worked with a magnifying glass and tiny brushes. Most of his representational paintings were of flowers, pretty and pastoral. Later, in 1943, before the Warsaw insurrection, on the Aryan side in hiding, he taught me everything I still know about anatomy and geography with his drawings.

On that occasion in the Ghetto, when he was in so much pain and drew me the happy picture of pacifism, I was very sad. I knew he was seriously hurt and in pain; he had been gone and returned broken. I remember my mother distraught because he was gone. His brother, Badza, had become a Jewish policeman and came with news; my mother fell on the floor weeping when Badza told her the news. That image lives in my head. Later, I found out he had been held by the Gestapo for three days and had been tortured and beaten. His brother somehow got him out. His body was broken for evermore. He lived most of his life with a huge hernia from that episode and refused to have it repaired until just before his death at sixty-four. My father died without ever talking about what the Gestapo did to him.

There was another terrible day that must have been before Yom Kippur 1942, because I know that by the time of the final selection at the Umschlagplatz, they were all gone. That day, too, my uncle Badza came running and my mother and father, taking me along, rushed off in a panic after him, to a thick column of people being herded with whips under armed guard, to a waiting train. My grandparents (my father's parents) and my mother's sisters and their husbands, all my aunts and uncles, except for Uncle Badza, had been taken and were being loaded into the waiting cattle car of the train.

They all had suitcases or heavy bundles of possessions with them. At that time, many people still believed that this was a resettlement rather than a trip to the ovens. My mother wept and grieved for her much-loved sisters and my father's parents. "They are going to their deaths," she cried. She said the resettlement and labor camp story was a lie, a vicious ruse calculated to accomplish less resistance; she raged and cried so passionately and begged the guards, but she was powerless.

. . .

That tragic, chaotic, dark, lamentable, tortured image of the sad, sad train station, of incredible, cruel inhumanity, lives in my mind, in picture and in sound. I wish I could excise it onto a dark canvas that would continue to bear witness when I am gone to dust.

. . .

My father and Uncle Badza stood by nearby and cried quietly; there was nothing they could do. Then my uncle Badza rushed off, saying he knew what to do. And we never saw him again. I asked my father about him later, when we were in a bunker on the Aryan side and the bombs were falling. My father said that he heard that Uncle Badza had gone to the forest to fight; he said Badza was big and strong so perhaps he would live.

After that, whenever we saw people with their suitcases and bundles, driven through the streets of the Ghetto to the trains, my mother would cry and rail that in this way the greedy murderers caused people to go with less resistance and bring their most prized and valuable possessions with them so they could then be most easily ripped away from them.

CHAPTER 4

The Aryan Side

After the Umschlagplatz, what I do remember in movement, images, smells, and feelings is when my mother took me out of the Ghetto and left me. I remember the guard hut at the exit that we had to cross. My mother had been to the Aryan side. She was so brave and strong of body and mind that she made that perilous journey every day, at that time, with false papers as a member of a Polish labor gang coming in to do forced labor in the Ghetto. That's how we all lived, on the scraps of food she managed to get past the guards into the ghetto from the Aryan side, risking her life every time she crossed, hidden behind her nerves of steel and her lifesaving bravado.

In order to save me, she acquired money through the black market and bribed certain guards at that crossing to let us through. I remember the feel and look of the "brama" building entranceway, where we stood by nonchalantly, standing as if we belonged there, to make sure no one noticed us. My mother instructed me, in that spot, at that time, on the most important lesson of survival. I must carefully, always remember these instructions: never look scared and always pretend to be occupied doing something fun, because if you want to make sure that people don't notice you, don't ask you questions, you must look occupied, nonchalant; but the most important was to never look afraid.

Not to look fearful was hard for me then because I was upset by the parting from my father just before we walked to the gate. My father was terrified that he would never see me again and communicated this to me in the parting embrace, which was so tight that it hurt me. I felt that he did not want to let me go. My mother forced him. This parting embrace with him, filled with terror, also filled me with such profound dread that the horror of it became part of my body, an ingrained memory which rose to the surface whenever my father tried to show me affection by holding me tight. To the end of his life, I was not able to tolerate this form of affection from my father, but I was not able to tell him how I remembered that event and why I experienced terror instead of love in his arms. This caused me to be withdrawn from him, which I know caused him pain and which now causes me pain, that deep ache of regret that can never be relieved.

. . .

There are so many things in my life, deeds of mine, mainly done out of compulsions that I still do not fully understand, that I so intensely rue, lament, and deplore. That feeling of deep regret is bound up with the huge boulder of sadness emanating from these mournful times that I have spent a good part of my life trying to escape, deny, and avoid by distancing myself from my past and finding other compulsions and preoccupations. In retrospect, however, it seems to me that the repetition compulsion reigned supreme in my life; avoidance and denial, such hard work in vain . . . this to me is the true meaning of the absurdity of life . . . the labors of Sisyphus.

. . .

I was five and a half years old when my mother and I non-chalantly strolled through that gate, past the guard, and on to the other side. It was during that stroll that I learned the most important lesson of survival: what to do to not look afraid even when I was terrified.

. . .

The trick was simple . . . I learnt it for life: do not be afraid by putting the fear away through intense distraction by something, anything, desirable. This became a major current of my life from then on: a love and frequent indulgence in markedly counter-pho-bic behavior in almost everything I actually chose to do. The more afraid I was, the more I loved the activity, was compelled to pursue it to excess, and could not stop.

. . .

Returning to my chronology of these hard times. It was late fall 1942, I was holding my mother's hand, and she was prompting me under her breath to look up, smile, look around, do not fear, do not run, walk slowly in pace with her. Thus we crossed to the Aryan side, turned onto a long street along the wall, and now began to walk more quickly, I having a hard time keeping up. But I knew it was important to leave the Ghetto gate behind us and move away, as if we had nothing to do with it. It was a warm and sunny day, but my mother had dressed me in all the clothes she could find—in layers and with a coat on top—because I was not coming back. I was going to be left on the Aryan side. As we walked, my mother instructed me in my new identity and required behavior. The main rules were:

never show fear, always look happy, avoid being questioned whenever possible, but if you have to answer, do it happily and quickly.

My name was Teresa Matuszewska; I was a Catholic named after a very important saint whose anniversary was in January. So that was my birthday. I had to learn all about my fictitious family, uncles and aunts, brothers and sisters, their names and looks; where I came from, address, and so on. My mother reassured me in case I forgot something: it was acceptable to get mixed up sometimes—fantasy was better than nothing. Soon we came upon a pastry shop. That was an experience I shall never forget.

We went inside the pastry shop and I was truly awed by the aroma of fresh, sweet dough and the sight of so many beautiful things to eat. There were other people, women not children, in the small space of the shop. I was so hot at this point that my coat had to come off. I felt the rivulets of sweat run down my cheeks. My mother took the ragged coat from me and put it on an available part of the counter; then a terrible thing happened. We were on the Aryan side, but I still had the mandatory Jewish emblem, the yellow Star of David, sewn onto my coat, as was required by German law for every Jew. But we were on the Aryan side where no Jews were allowed and I was Teresa Matuszewska, a baptized Christian, a Polish child. The Star of David was visible right on top as my coat lay on that counter. I felt the fear from my mother as I saw her see the damning emblem. But, accomplished, brave survivor that she always was, she kept her cool, never looked in that direction again, bought me an unforgettable pastry, a mille feuilles, Polish-style, brimming with custard that she later told me had more nutrition than just sugar and dough, picked up the coat, rolling up the star to the inside quickly and adroitly, making it invisible.

I do not know why she put that ragged, lice-ridden little garment on the counter. I wish we had been able to talk about those times and I had asked her. But we could not, I did not, and I don't know. Perhaps it was a part of her survival nonchalance to throw it there, or she needed to do it to pay for the pastry. In any case, it was one of those wartime moments when courage and luck conspired to aid us to live through the terror. We walked away as quickly as possible, without looking back, and then laughed uproariously together with happiness at the narrow escape. Looking back was one of those fearful gestures my mother taught me never to do.

. . .

This incident is a perfect example of how exciting, pleasurable, and addictive that kind of danger was for me. Laughter with my mother was repeated many times as a response to extreme danger outwitted and outbluffed. I believe that I have searched for that closeness and happiness throughout my life by putting myself at risk as much as I could. For some reason, though, that I find obscure and impenetrable, I am not suicidal at all in the normal sense of that word. Instead, what I do is put in extreme jeopardy the part or aspect of my life that is most important and precious to me in that manifestation of my life (and I do not say "manifestation" lightly—indeed it would be almost more accurate to say metamorphosis, "another, virtually unrelated life"). For example, when I was married to my first husband, Bill Thompson, a very talented and committed scientist, a biochemist who loved science, music, and his many friends in the academic community, I was the perfect academic wife, running the household for gentlemanly British dinner parties followed by bridge games and scientific discussions in which I schooled myself to intelligently participate. My Jewishness was pushed away and disguised as much as possible. I lived a lie: that the years here chronicled and these experiences did not scar me and were not adversely formative. Even if I was traumatized then, I acted as though I had totally recovered. I played a stiff-upper-lip role in that life and I was not my genuine self. I was Jean-Paul Sartre's perfect waiter: the existential academic wife, without any historical baggage or lament.

A necessary part of the super-risk scenario that I was addicted to and had to live out in some form was an element of hiding, or a dangerous secret to be protected at all cost. This made me a liar, so I could, with good reason, hate myself. I was truly an adrenaline junkie, needing a very special combination to relieve the anxiety created by loss. Perhaps this was not as rigid as a fetish, in content. Nonetheless, it absolutely required the two elements—of self-destructive risk and secrecy or hiding—in order to give me relief, by launching me on a quest for that sense of ease and happiness I experienced in childhood in those moments of emotional closeness I craved.

Every major loss in my life, except my mother's death, caused in me an extreme anxiety that could only be relieved by the adrenaline high of secrecy plus serious risk. I believe these were the dynamics of my lifetime of self-destructive patterns, including my gambling addiction, that I pushed as close as possible to an annihilation of myself. I did, in fact, succeed in destroying the shape and means of my life, my persona and self-esteem, that I had worked so hard to build. I ended my legal career ignominiously, depriving myself of a much-needed livelihood; I had destroyed already, with a prior compulsion containing these very elements, the love and trust in my second marriage to the father of my daughter; and I came within a hair of also losing my partner's love and my daughter's love. Without them, I would not have, and could not have, survived as a whole human being in yet another very different manifestation of my life, another metamorphosis. I was less than a Pavlovian dog in my complete inability to control my behavior in response to the anxiety created by loss. But the final loss of my mother was different.

My mother's death was a loss so painful for me I could not even take it in, but over an extended period of time. I could not mourn and weep right away, especially because, since my mother was gone, I felt I had to take on the nonchalant survivor role in relation to my daughter, to protect her, and could not show the pain. But my mother's death left me with so much lament buried in that impenetrable, fathomless, cavernous sense of grief and regret that any occasion of even passing sadness, or random event recalling her, would bring tears to my eyes.

Many months later, Jeff's father, Simone's grandfather, died; I wept uncontrollably throughout the long ceremony, in good part, I believe, for my mother. It's not that I did not mourn for Jacques; I had loved him and I did cry over his loss, but I used it also as a permissible occasion to weep, and so I wept for my mother too. I had not really allowed myself to weep for her directly because I was afraid that my immense sorrow, once unleashed, would overwhelm me totally.

For my mother, we had only a small ceremony. Simone and I went to a rabbi who was kind enough to try to teach us the Kaddish, even though we knew no Hebrew. We gave her a send-off at home, both of us, I believe, afraid to mourn, as if to do so would bring up too much suffering. My mother's death was very hard for Simone to bear because she had so adored her bubbe. My mother loved "the child" and stepped in to mother her, to cover her with affection when I was not available to my child because I was lost in my compulsions.

To mourn my mother was to mourn a whole way of life destroyed, a whole people murdered, and a language and culture gone forever, a genocide truly accomplished. Thus we did what we could and it was not much. Simone and I said Kaddish for my mother. For me, it was also my Kaddish for all those murdered, for all those lost, loved grandparents, aunts, uncles, cousins, friends that I had not been able to mourn yet. I carry within me a sad lament for my mother and I rue that unhappy distance from her that I could not bridge in her lifetime; tortured grief often erupts in tears and overwhelms me with feelings of having let her down and of having destroyed the laughter and closeness I so craved. Now that she is gone, it is too late to recapture the easy, joyful happiness I experienced so many times with her, of overcoming powerful and brutal enemies by ruse and wit; and of cheating death at the last moment. Yet, oddly, her death somehow freed me of the compulsions that had wrecked so much of my life.

. . .

My mother's very best friend for many years, Halina Gebasz, was a very blond, strong, tall, young Polish woman. She was an atheist not a Catholic, very brave, a member of the PPS, the Polish Socialist Party, and an armed member of the resistance during the war, who truly saved all of us. My mother stayed with her whenever she was on the Aryan side. Halina is the one who obtained my various identities, my father's hiding place, his Aryan identity, Jan Kowalewski (the identity he retained, in that so very Polish name, to the end of his life), and always papers for my mother. It is Halinka who got my mother into the Polish labor gang so she could funnel to us life and food in the dying Ghetto. It is to Halinka's that my mother led me from the Ghetto.

I know it was a very long walk and I felt very tired, especially as we walked quickly all the way. My mother kept me going by promising the wonderful pastry at the end. Finally, we arrived. Halina and my mother greeted each other with a warm embrace. Halina kissed me too and said how pretty and grown-up I looked, but I could see she was worried. I heard them talking later about how Jewish I looked. My mother said she knew what to do: she would say that I was the child of a Jew and a Catholic and that I had been baptized. I wondered what it all meant, but I knew there was danger ahead. Then, at last, I ate my very first pastry, so quickly that it literally disappeared, even though it was huge, almost as big as my whole face. It must have been delicious, but I don't remember the taste. Perhaps I swallowed too quickly to taste.

Then came the worst part of the visit. I had lice, as did everyone in the Ghetto. It was a sure giveaway. Everyone would know. So the lice had to be destroyed. That's how Halina explained it to me as my mother held me affectionately, ready to help. The procedure was painful and unpleasant. As Halina worked on me, my mother told me everything she was doing and why. My hair, tangled from being braided, was soaked in evil-smelling kerosene, then combed through to remove the dead lice. The combing felt like the hair was being torn out but I stayed quiet and did not cry. My mother and Halina praised me for being so brave. I know that I did not want to leave the aura of strength, cheerfulness, and protection that I felt from Halinka, and from my mother, in her environment. It was so different from the heavy, sombre, horror-filled tones of the Ghetto. Instinctively, I knew that only sadness and fear awaited me away from that haven.

When it came time to leave, my mother explained to me that I could not stay there because it was too dangerous to have me around. It did not fit her identity or Halina's. I would be recognized as a Jewish child and then everyone would be murdered. I understood then that I must hide who I truly was at all costs and that I could not be with anyone I loved or who loved me. It was too dangerous.

And so we left, my mother and I. My mother looked so sad and apprehensive, I remember, but tried hard to maintain her nonchalant, carefree way to make sure no one suspected anything as we walked across Warsaw. I adored my mother. She looked so beautiful to me. I thought she was the most wonderful and the most beautiful person in the world, and I wanted to be as close as possible to her all the time. I remember every detail of her face then, as I looked up at her or stole glances from the side. Thinking about it now, I realize that she was a striking beauty. I remember that people often stared at her, perhaps because her beauty had a soft, appealing quality; maybe the sadness under the survival-studied nonchalance added a little mystery and made her even more intriguing.

As we walked and walked, I was getting very tired and had a sense of foreboding about what was to come; in a way,

I knew—I had heard so many snippets of frightening conversation. I wanted our walk to continue forever. But, finally, we arrived. We went into the internal courtyard of a building, inside a stairwell, and up a flight of stairs to a doorway that soon opened into a very small apartment. Many years later, in another life, I discovered it was called a "but 'n' ben" in Glasgow, another city of tenements.

. . .

I am trying to avoid writing about this most painful of all events of the war for me, by wandering off to Glasgow, where I went as the perfect wife of Dr. Thompson, many years later, in another life.

. . .

Back to Warsaw, 1942. An old woman lived in that two-room apartment. She looked harsh and angular, and I was afraid of her. My mother asked me a few questions and I answered dutifully, knowing I had now become Teresa Matuszewska. The old woman's name was Pani Masło (Mrs. Butter). She and my mother went into the other room while I waited anxiously in the kitchen, by the stove. Pani Masło had a little German dachshund that she did not introduce to me, who was lying on a bed in the kitchen, covered with a nice warm knitted blanket, evidently where her owner slept.

When my mother returned to the kitchen, she was crying. She knelt down by me, took me in her arms, stroked me lovingly, and told me the dreaded truth. I was to stay with Pani Masło, to live with her, to be good and obey her always. My mother said that she had to leave to take care of my father; it was too dangerous for her to stay and that I would be much safer with Pani Masło, but that she would come and see me and visit from time to time. She asked me not to cry to help her leave. And I did not, but as soon as she left the sobs escaped from me and I could not stop a wail or two even though Pani Masło told me to stop immediately because of the neighbors.

I was crushed, so sad, so afraid; I felt totally alone and bereft. A leaden melancholy enveloped me and I began to shiver with a hurting cold. Pani Masło then took me into the other room, the parlor, and showed me my bed: it was the bottom drawer of the *szafa*, a big wardrobe. She told me that the drawer was both my hiding place and my sleeping space and that I should be absolutely quiet in there to make sure no one heard me. I got in and lay down, curled up. I was so cold and I remember thinking enviously of the little dog with his blanket near the warmth of the stove. I was still crying very quietly for my beautiful, loving mother, gone. And I was very, very cold, with a chill that permeated to the core of me.

My mother did come to visit me. But the time between the visits stretched on forever, and when she was gone I did not know if I would ever see her again. I spent my time at Pani Masło's mainly in my drawer. I never did get a blanket, so I was cold there most of the time; I was out of sight, out of mind, away from trouble. On Sundays, though, I had to come out. Pani Masło felt it was her duty to save my soul and insisted on taking me to church. I hated going to church with Pani Masło. I hated Pani Masło. She was very rough with me and would smack me hard and unexpectedly across the side of the head whenever she looked at me and I was not absolutely correct in how I walked down the street next to her. If I lost the step, looked down, looked around, let my attention wander, or looked a little apprehensive, the smack would come fast and hard. Any cry, even the slightest whimper, would immediately cause another stinging slam.

One day, all the way back from the church, I cried and whimpered in my motherless sorrow. I felt Pani Masło's anger building beside me. She told me that I would receive the punishment I deserved as soon as we arrived home. I would have to be completely silent to make the punishment stop. I was afraid of Pani Masło so I tried to stop, but I could not. As soon as we were inside, Pani Masło shut and locked the door. She turned to me and slapped me very hard across the face. Then she put me across her lap and beat me as hard as she could with her open hand.

Finally, one day, I woke up in my drawer and an exciting, soft, and tingling joy bathed me from head to toe as, very faintly, I heard my mother's voice calling to me almost in a whisper. Then, slowly and quietly, the drawer was pulled out and I was staring joyfully at my mother's beautiful face. Oh, how wonderful it was to find myself in my mother's arms, loved and protected. It lasted such a short time, though. Pani Masło quickly reminded her that it was very dangerous to all of us for her to be here, with me. My mother realized she had to leave; she quickly gave Pani Masło some money and a necklace, me some last kisses and a big hug. And she was gone; my horrible life with the devout, loveless, harsh Pani Masło resumed immediately.

I know that my mother came to see me several times in the year and a half or so that I lived with Pani Masło. But one day, I had another visitor: I woke up suddenly, afraid. Voices had awakened me. I looked up into a face at least partly hidden behind a bristly moustache and tried to curl into the drawer with fear. It was my father. I had not seen him since the Ghetto and did not recognize him in the dim and strange surroundings of Pani Masło's parlor. But as he began to speak to me softly and lovingly, as he had in the past, my fear dissolved and I stretched up towards him lovingly as he lifted me into his arms.

I see him now standing there, his clothes hanging on a skeletal body, and I wonder how he had the strength to lift me, especially with the hernia that must have hurt. I suppose that I was pretty thin, small, and light too.

One thing I remember very clearly and aromatically is the smell of tobacco that emanated from my father on that occasion. Tobacco was the most prized possession in those days; an unobtainable luxury. Both my mother and father and everyone else *ex nostris*, as my mother used to say, smoked and obtained their cigarettes the same way: by scouring the streets for thrown away butts, no matter how small, then carefully opening them to save even the tiniest dreg, and rolling the crumbled dried tobacco into a piece of newspaper. That's what they smoked at every opportunity of respite with such immense pleasure that, of course, I wanted a taste and got it. I must have liked it because I always thought of cigarettes as extremely good and desirable and started smoking as soon as I could.

One day, I now know that it was May 16, 1943, my mother came to see me at Pani Masło's drab abode, unable to disguise her grief and sadness. Outside, the sky was dark with heavy black smoke. I do not remember how we got to the Ghetto wall. But there we were. The scene is deeply etched in my memory. A crowd, five or six deep, had gathered along the wall. Many people were laughing and jeering. Others watched dumbstruck by the site of the immense fire. It seemed that every building inside the Ghetto was burning, some spurting thick black smoke, others aflame; there were explosions of smoke and flames too, with sparks flying. My mother lifted me so I could see and whispered to me that this was the greatest tragedy of all time and that we were watching a terrible evil. I know that was the first time she told me that we must survive to tell what happened. That apocalyptic image of death and destruction, of black smoke pierced by tongues of dark red fire, the crackle and boom, sparks, and collapsing buildings, lives still in my mind, etched forever into my memory.

My mother, it seems, had news about me, perhaps through Halina, even when she was not with me. I presume this was so because one day she came with the happy news that we were leaving Pani Masło's together, never to return. She told me that it had become too dangerous because people had seen me and were talking about me being a Jewish child. This was very dangerous because someone might give me away.

I was very happy to hear the news that this time, finally, I would not be left behind. That is all I cared about then, and I was so happy that I could hardly contain my joy to sit quietly while my mother concluded her business with Pani Masło. I was ecstatic when we finally said goodbye and left that drab building and the dark, meager, joyless surroundings of Mrs. Masło's life forever.

. . .

I was five years old in that year or so with Pani Masło. Nonetheless, that experience continues to affect my life in ways that I know have to do with my lifelong desire to distance and separate myself from this experience: I hate and refuse to use curtains because they darken rooms; I love the noise of laughter and tears, of human emotions; I like demonstrative affection; I like color and beauty in everything in daily life; I have a distaste for and a fear of the dark moodiness of suppressed anger; I am intensely averse to all things, ideas, ways of life, drab. I fear drabness most of all.

. . .

My happiness at leaving Pani Masło was soon interrupted by fear and unease as to what awaited me next when my mother told me that I was to be left alone in a new identity on a small farm very near Warsaw. She then quickly set about schooling me in my new persona. I was still Teresa, Terenia, Tereska, but now Kowalska, with a whole new set of parents, aunts, and uncles, and two brothers, Jurek and Jerzyk. My mother tried very hard and eventually succeeded in making me a little happier and more cheerful about my approaching lonely fate by telling me tales of all the wonderful little animals on the farm: little rabbits, piglets, chicks, ducks, dogs, and cats. We took a streetcar to the outskirts of the city, then waited a while until a horse-and-buggy picked us up. I was so thrilled at riding in the buggy that, for a little while, I forgot my weighty troubles and felt my eyes grow wide with wonder and my spirits lift up high. I have loved the smell of horses since then. But life on the little farm was not the idyllic haven that my mother had wishfully hinted at for me. On the contrary, life on the farm was violent, hard, and cruel.

Every day, I had to go out and run with a band of children, all of whom were bigger and stronger than scrawny, emaciated, and undernourished me. The play was rough and frightening to me. Until that point in my life I had never played with other children; and much of the play consisted of jeering at me, because of my looking like a Jewess, probably being a worthless, disgusting Jewess, and threats of the terrible things that would befall me if my true identity were discovered or revealed.

Then something very painful for me happened.

Of all the animals on the farm, I loved the rabbits most of all. They were so gentle, so soft, so tender. I loved them all. There were three. But I loved the beautiful, black-and-white rabbit most of all. He was my rabbit and I loved to rub my face in his soft fur. Then, one day, my very first friend whom I loved unconditionally and without restraint, my black-and-white rabbit, was no more: he was served for dinner. I remember with painful clarity being told, "To jest twoj maly na objad dzisaj" (It's your little one for dinner today). I refused to understand and I ran out to look for my rabbit. I ran everywhere and looked for a long time, but to no avail. The darkness of night fell.

After a good while, my mother came to visit; but when she saw what a terrible state I was in and heard about the rough games and the jeering, she said: "It has become much too dangerous here. We have to leave." Then she and I spent a sleepless night and left the next day. That night, I found out what a bedbug was: I was covered with sores because I had scratched raw the hundreds of bedbug bites all over my body. During the night, my mother picked out of the wall and off the bed several bedbugs and showed me how to kill them, like lice, between your nails.

Again, I was happy to leave, but very apprehensive about the next place, and so sad that I would be left alone, abandoned, and bereft once more. It was a very long walk, no horse-and-buggy to take us back. In retrospect, I wonder if my mother had run out of money, perhaps, and that's why we were walking. She used the time with me to teach me my next identity. I know I learned it well because I remember my mother's astonishment and praise at how quickly I absorbed all of the details of my new Catholic persona and answered all her questions correctly. I was so proud.

For many years, I refused to acknowledge what had happened to the rabbit, but always felt a deep sorrow and a sharply painful loneliness when I saw a rabbit like mine. It was not until many years later, looking back, that I was actually able to admit what had occurred. I still find it hard to think about.

A dreadful aspect of daily life on the Aryan side in wartime Warsaw for Jews was the terror of *lapanki*, which literally translates to "catchings." The Germans or their brutal helpers—Lithuanians of the feared Wlasow Army, or fascist Ukrainians, or virulently antisemitic Polish policemen—set up barricades and examined, questioned, and scrutinized the papers of everyone who passed, arresting people at random if they suspected anything.

Lapanki were extremely dangerous, to be avoided at all costs. They occurred suddenly and unpredictably, all over Warsaw, but very often at tramway stops, or actually inside the trams. For that reason, my very resourceful and agile mother would never board a streetcar while it was stopped and rarely remained inside to a full stop. Always on watch and aware of possible traps and dangers, my mother's means of survival required that we jump on while the streetcar was in full motion and exit the same way. That meant running alongside quickly enough to make the leap. In 1943 and 1944, when this was occurring in my life, I was five and six years old and obviously capable of this feat, since I always made it on and off with my mother. But I know now that I was terrified of not being able to keep up.

Riding a streetcar in wartime Warsaw with my mother was an adventure and a hard lesson from her in itself, and often repeated and preserved in my dreams to this day.

. . .

The fear was encapsulated in a terrifying, recurring dream that I had for many years, but thankfully have not had for a long time. In this dream, my mother and I are being pursued; we are running for our lives. Onto a moving streetcar, off the streetcar while it is moving very fast (that terrified me). But years later in Paris too, in Lille, in Amsterdam, with intense counter-phobic verve, that was the only way I would ever get on and off streetcars. In North America, I developed a phobia of public transportation because that means of access and exit did not exist and I felt so trapped that I could not sustain the anxiety and would have to get off. The dream continued into what is a memory of getting in and out of hiding places; it was difficult for me as a child; I know that I always feared I would not be fast enough. In the dream, after the scary jumping on and off the moving streetcars, I had to follow my mother very rapidly under difficult-to-lift floorboards or underneath some other hard to access concealment.

My phobia of public transportation, on the ground, has remained with me; but if I really try, I can combat it if absolutely necessary. Oddly, it does not extend to flying. On the contrary. I love flying, providing, that is, that I can have an aisle seat. I realize that this makes absolutely no sense. How and where would I escape to from my aisle seat on an airplane in flight? Unfortunately, understanding the irrationality helps a little, but it does not wipe out the anxiety.

I do not suffer from existential angst; I do not have a melancholic turn of mind. Mine are very personal anxieties, the result of memories deeply repressed, trauma manifesting in this odd garb.

. . .

When I think about life on the Aryan side in wartime Warsaw, I realize now why it was always my mother who went about, did errands, took streetcars, and moved around in the city doing what was necessary for life, while my father left his hiding place only very rarely, as infrequently as possible. This was because it was so much more dangerous for Jewish men; the population was so culturally and religiously homogenous that male Jews could be instantly identified by virtue of being circumcised. No Polish males were circumcised. That form of degrading identification occurred frequently, all over Warsaw, in the shadows of the entrances to buildings, by brutish, bullying, murderously antisemitic Poles hoping for some small favor or reward for a Jewish life.

In the summer of 1944, after I turned seven years old, I went to live with my father in his hiding place. This was because my father heard that the Warsaw Uprising was about to start and my father persuaded my mother that, even though it was very dangerous because we did not have the documents to support it, it was better than being separated in the chaos of fighting, never to see each other again. "From now on," my father insisted repeatedly, "we must stay together at all costs, against all odds." I do not think that my mother really agreed; she was scared of what might happen to me, but she gave in to my father because he was so passionately certain that he was right. And so it was that I stayed with my father all day while my mother went about Warsaw acquiring bits of food for us and trying to keep in touch with those very few still alive.

Even though the apartment was up two stories, the windows looked down upon the courtyard where children played and where, sometimes, neighbors stood about, chatting and smoking. To keep our privacy complete, because any kind of exposure was so dangerous, the curtains were always drawn and I was not allowed to stand by the window lest someone glimpse me from below. I longed to go down and run and play with the other children, but I was also afraid to be seen, terrified of exposure; so I pushed down my childish longing to be a child and learnt the skills of survival. My father was wonderful to be with compared to the various other caretakers, like Pani Masło, that I had endured; he taught me to read from newspapers, and so much more from his drawings. Even though his drawings were mostly in blue pen, he talked about them in color and taught me a love and sensitivity for the transposition of color and shape.

One day, a neighbor from a building across the courtyard must have seen me in the corner of the forbidden window, trying to catch a glimpse of community life and play in the courtyard below, something I was not allowed to do, but sometimes just couldn't resist. She must have seen me, because, aggressively, full of suspicion, she blocked us in the stairwell before we could disappear behind the door and, addressing me, began an interrogation about who I was and where I had come from. I remember the knot of fear in the pit of my stomach as the questions began. Then, all of a sudden, my imagination, unafraid and free as a bird, so well-schooled in survival by my mother's lessons and example, answered all the questions with perfect embellishment and such an accomplished carefree air that we knew we had won again. As soon as the door had closed behind us, my mother held me tight; we laughed and she whispered her praise and approval to me. My father, too, heard the story and praised my wit and resourcefulness to the heavens.

. . .

When I think about this scene now, I see this Polish woman clearly. Sadly, I recognize that I too survived these despairing events marked by bitter, inappropriate bigotries, no less dangerous because they are mine. I can still feel that fear combined with a sensation of utter distaste and dislike for the uncompassionate, insensitive Polish woman, almost certainly a devout Christian, filled with hatred and cruelty, probably fed from the pulpit every Sunday. I see that Polish woman now in that old and dirty staircase, aggressive and threatening, trying to wield venomous power over other human beings she perceived to be weaker. I see her as physically possessing all the characteristics I find, still, most unattractive: flaxen, dirty blond hair, washed-out pale blue eyes, the heavy, stodgy demeanor of a well-fed, big person towering over me.

. . .

One day, my father and I, like two naughty children, alone in the apartment, were not where we were supposed to stay most of the time—in the small, airless, difficult hiding place between the ceiling and the next floor, accessed through the ceiling in a hallway. Instead, we were sitting together at a small table in the main room, by the window, which was a thrill even though the curtains were drawn. My father was drawing the anatomy of a hand for me, when we heard a huge racket, a banging at the courtyard gate, then orders shouted in German and soldiers marching loudly up the stairs to our door. We were startled, overcome with terror. I saw my father look about for a place to hide, and finding nothing, he took my hand, pulled me into the back room, furthest away from the front door. We heard the violent sound of the front door collapsing from the force of boots and gun butts just as we made it under the only cover available, under the two beds in the room. I knew instinctively, as my father let go of my hand, that I had to go under one bed and he under the other. I remember that I felt fear, but not extreme terror; I felt fear mixed with excitement, almost as if I knew that we were not done for this time. We heard the loud march of boots throughout the apartment, the cracking, banging, and breaking sounds of searching, and finally the very loud bang as the small phalanx of soldiers, accompanied by the sergeant shouting orders, pushed in the door and marched into the room where we were hiding. At that moment, I must have turned my head slightly toward the noise and saw my father's feet sticking out from under the bed. Luckily, the phalanx was so well trained as to march with heads up, looking straight ahead, and saw nothing on the ground. They simply smashed through everything with gun butts, touching nothing out of an inordinate fear of disease, and having thus smashed through the whole place, we soon heard the final *achtung* and with the same loud banging and fast march as when they arrived, they were gone.

This incident in our wartime adventures was the subject of great and continuing hilarity for many years to come. It was told over and over again as the perfect example of the triumph of Jewish nerve, wit, and ingenuity over the witless, brutish power of the enemy. It was also used, accompanied by hilarity, as an illustration of how unquestioning obedience, the Germanic adulation for following orders, is a characteristic of thick, ignorant people, incapable of independent judgment, not of good, intelligent people, able to think and argue.

. . .

These are the deep lessons of my childhood that form the actual substance of my person, like bone and muscle form the body. To remove them is impossible without surgery.

How then can I think of Jews as the powerful aggressors against others; Jews building a wall to contain and destroy another people? I simply cannot think about it without tearing myself apart and without a painful sadness that my mind rejects and feels as a betrayal of my mother's and my legacy.

CHAPTER 5

Powązki

Sometime in the early summer of 1943, for a reason I cannot now remember, my mother and I, on one of those jaunts across Warsaw that I loved so much because it was just the two of us laughing together at escaping from whatever dangers we encountered, were walking up Powązki Street, when suddenly I felt my mother freeze in her tracks, as if she had seen a ghost; I looked up to see what had so startled her and saw a very well dressed gentleman coming toward us. I felt that he was looking at us very intently, but at the same time, I realized that he was trying to appear as if he had not seen us at all, as if he was not looking at us. As he came past, I heard him whisper to my mother. She was leaning over me, fussing with my dress, as he walked by. "It's Uncle Marek," my mother whispered to me. "We will follow him to the cemetery, where we can talk." And so we did.

Uncle Marek had a newspaper with him. He walked past us and we turned and followed him at a considerable distance to make sure our tryst remained secret. After he entered the cemetery, he sat down on a shady bench and unfolded his newspaper so he was almost entirely hidden behind it. We sat down next to him, and he and my mother exchanged news about who had been taken or murdered and who was still alive. Uncle Marek was happy to hear that my father was still safe; tears streamed down his face at the fate of my father's parents and their whole family, and my mother's parents and sisters; my mother wept when she heard that Marek's wife, two young daughters, and the entire Rosenbaum family had been taken. But we could not stay long. Someone might come by and suspect. Uncle Marek (whom I called "uncle" because he was a familial older male; he was my father's cousin, not his brother, but they were close) squeezed my hand behind the newspaper and was gone, walking very quickly away and through the exit. A few minutes later we followed, my mother still very sad and wrapped up in her thoughts.

I remember at least one other occasion when I was in the cemetery at Powązki. It was one of the few occasions, in fact the only one that I remember, when my mother, my father, and I, all three of us, dared to take the risk of walking the streets of Warsaw together. It was somehow all arranged by my mother on one of those trysts all over Warsaw that she arranged every day, in search of food, cigarette butts, and people—to keep track of who was alive and to send and receive secret messages. So it was that as a result of her efforts, we would be meeting in the cemetery, Jurek, now thirteen or fourteen years old, tall and strong, now a committed member of the Polish resistance, and my Uncle Marek, whom my father wanted very much to see; they had been close, like brothers, and Marek was the only remaining member of my father's family still alive.

When we arrived, walking down the long central path, Marek Rosenbaum Majewski (Majewski was Marek's very Polish war name that, like my father, he kept after the war, to the end of his days) was already there, reading a newspaper, sitting casually on a bench. Before the war, Marek was wealthy and did not need to work. He was a collector of art and a very fine photographer. He had a small camera with him that Sunday afternoon in the Powązki cemetery, in the summer of 1944; it was he who took some of the pictures that now accompany *My Kaddish*, this tale of good against evil fought so hard and won by my mother's indomitable spirit and my father's odd, unusual gentleness.

· · ·

The price of that victory, of my very existence, so hard fought and hard won, is not negligible; it is paid by me, throughout my life, with pain, and paid too by all those who love me now and loved me in the past, and who suffered from my wounded and deeply scarred ability to love and to relate: my husbands, my partner, and most of all my daughter, whom I could not mother as totally as I wanted to and as she needed. But she too is a survivor and has grown, much on her own, into a beautiful and compassionate woman. When I am gone, she will be the sole survivor carrying on her Bubbe's splendid legacy.

· · ·

Back to my mournful tale—Warsaw, summer 1944 in Powązki cemetery. Uncle Marek took everyone's picture with his little camera; he and my father talked and talked; my mother nonchalantly walked up and down, toward the gate, keeping guard to make sure no one dangerous was approaching; and I ran about with Jurek, having a wonderful time, proud of his kindness and constant attention. On the farm, though he was not especially cruel to me and sometimes even tried to protect me a little against real physical harm, he was a member of that gang that tortured me daily. Now he was here, my friend, and with me.

Most exciting of all were the stories he told me of the fight against the enemy in which he would soon participate. He was waiting and expected the order any day. Then he whispered to me the secret: where the arms and weapons were hidden for the great struggle. He told me that they were hidden inside the graves, here at Powązki. I have always believed this unquestionably. It is only now as I write this that I wonder for the first time: Was this really true? Is there a way to check more than sixty years later? Should I check? Why didn't I find out last year, on the sixtieth anniversary of the Warsaw Uprising, when I was in Warsaw with Simone. It was my very first trip to Poland since these sad events took place.

One day during that trip to Warsaw last summer, just a day or two before we had to leave, there was a real downpour, almost like a tropical storm. It was certainly too wet to wander through the city on foot, as we had been doing, tracing the Ghetto wall, trying to take in the sights and sounds of what had been and how little remained, and trying to keep our composure and balance in that sea of swirling emotions. We were driving when, suddenly, staring out of the passenger window, I happened to see the street sign for Powązki Street. It was a true déjà vu and came to me complete with the memory of staring at that sign when I was a little girl, when I had to look up a long way and was just learning to read from everything my eyes encountered. All of a sudden, after sixty years and several lifetimes intervening, I knew exactly where I was in

Warsaw. Excitedly, I asked Simone to park the car as quickly as she could, and knowing just where to go, I led my daughter to Powązki cemetery. It was very exciting to be there again. I remembered first meeting Marek and could almost see him, sitting so casually behind his newspaper; I remembered Jurek and tried hard to find the right bench; that proved almost impossible: we had not brought the picture and none of the benches fitted our mental images exactly. Perhaps in sixty years simply too much changes naturally. I was particularly disappointed because I could not even pinpoint the graves that, as I was so delightfully told, contained those righteous resistance weapons waiting to teach the murderers a thing or two they so deserved. In Powązki, summer 1944, as I remembered the occasion, we still whispered these words to each other with excited exhilaration; soon, we promised each other, we will drive the murderers out of our land. There will be no more need for whispers.

CHAPTER 6

The Bunker

———

A month or two later, on August 1st, 1944, the Warsaw Uprising began. Jurek was one of the boys who manned a machine gun, one of the very few such weapons owned by the resistance, on a hill above Powązki. He died in a pitched battle with a German Panzer tank, on that hill sometime in September, before his fourteenth birthday. We heard about his death from Halina, after the war. She knew his parents.

I remember that after the start of the uprising and before the siege of Warsaw, when the German army with the aid of all their virulently antisemitic Eastern European allies, laid siege to the city and took it back house by house, street by street. Having been driven out of Warsaw, as they had been out of the Ghetto, by a bunch of boys and girls, mainly armed with a few pistols and a lot of Molotov cocktails, the Germans constantly and heavily bombed Warsaw from the air. I do not know now, and cannot remember if I ever knew, whether that bombing was by the Allies—the British and the US—against the occupying armies of the Reich, or by the Luftwaffe in aid of its army, against Warsaw. Whoever was bombing hit all over the city, and all around I remember seeing only ruins. Again, I am so mad, so sad that I was not able to talk to my mother to know what was actually happening.

We stayed in the bunker, crowded in with everyone else, too many people in a small area. I remember the horrible smell. Many people were afraid to go out at all as long as the bombs whistled and lived in the bunker for many days. My mother was not afraid, and once she even took me up through a ruined building to a bathroom with no walls. The shower worked. We both took a shower. I remember how exhilarated and free I felt to be up so high, without any enclosure. It seems to me now, as I look at the scene in my mind and recall the climb through the ruins, that we were up several stories, looking out over the ruins of Warsaw. I was so happy to feel the water run over my body. I felt so light and clean. Sometimes I felt that I could fly like the birds I saw in the sky; they were free to go anywhere, to go far away, and no one could catch them. I longed for that freedom.

. . .

I have retained the love of showering to this day. A good shower always makes me feel better. For many years, I loved cold showers. Now, I have gone to the other extreme and take very hot showers, so hot they seem unbearable, scalding to others. But I love that feeling of extreme temperature on my skin. Perhaps one temperature extreme is reminiscent of the other. I have also retained the longing to fly like a bird.

. . .

Another incident from my life in the bunker that I recall vividly is an image, up in the sky, that I experienced as an out-of-this-world, fantastically beautiful sight. In the bunker, I was surrounded by constant praying to a God who lived up in the heavens, above the sky, performed miracles, and sent signs and omens to people. What I saw when I looked up at a perfectly clear blue sky was a silvery glistening streak, flying high above me, much larger than a bird, nothing that I could identify, very beautiful and awesome. I ran back to the bunker, with great excitement, because I thought that I had seen a sign from God of something good because the image was so beautiful and so calm and the accompanying sounds of the whistling bombs so eerie.

My father was my primary teacher of intellectual matters, by word and by his wonderful illustrative drawings; my mother taught me how to live and to survive even in the midst of genocide by imaginative example. But my mother loved opera, and for some reason by connection to operatic librettos, she loved stories of Greek and Roman Gods. I knew the names and major functions of the Roman gods, especially, and in this experience I believe that I confused Jupiter with the Christian God that I heard about all around. I knew nothing about Judaism. That was far too dangerous a subject. Except that from the Ghetto I remembered some holidays and I knew the sadness of Yom Kippur. I also knew that the entire subject was forbidden because of the extreme danger associated with Jewishness.

Getting back to my first spiritual experience, my father explained the phenomenon I had seen as a shiny metal tramway track, torn up by a bomb and flung into the sky by the power of the explosion. He said he had seen the same image in the sky when he had gone outside when the bombs were whistling. And, yes, it was beautiful, like a wonderful painting. My mother, a little more tolerant of people's spiritual experiences, simply assured me that, for sure, it was not Jupiter.

This memorable incident occurred one day, during my life in the bunker; it was just like many other days that I remember when I needed to go to the bathroom. I waited until I saw that everyone was occupied and not looking; then I darted through the only opening to the outside world, into the completely deserted street and in behind some ruins, out of sight. I was timid and absolutely refused to go to the bathroom in the smelly bunker, in the midst of all its inhabitants crowding all around. My parents were afraid for me because of bombs and shrapnel and remonstrated with me each time. But I believe that they understood my need for that breath of fresh air and freedom, and I understood their tolerance, so I continued. Then came that day of Jupiter's thunderbolt in the sky that turned out to be just a flying shiny metal tramway track.

. . .

Oddly, that image and the entire memory came back to me in Tahiti, many years and many lives later when, talking to the beautiful, strong tribal women of those gorgeous outcroppings of coral in the middle of the blue South Pacific, I heard about the barracuda. These tribal women are the divers of the village, tending and protecting the oyster farms at the bottom of the reef wall. The women dive wearing masks only, not at all afraid of sharks; apparently the sharks in these waters are family minded and shy, but the barracuda with their dangerous, powerful tails cannot resist the glimmer of a shiny object in the deep. So it was in Tahiti, on a small island, literally not much more than an outcropping of coral, many worlds away, as far away as it is possible to get from the Warsaw Ghetto, that I suddenly found myself staring in my mind at that image I found so captivating and spellbinding as I ran about in the wartime ruins of Warsaw.

. . .

I do not know for how long we actually lived in the bunker, nor where it was, nor how we got there. I do remember with painful clarity, however, the end of that part of my story. It was after the Warsaw Uprising, when the German army, aided by its vicious Eastern European allies, as incredibly and brutally antisemitic, if not more so, as the Germans themselves, took the city back, having been driven out by that handful of kids with Molotov cocktails and a very few machine guns. The German army was effectively driven out of Warsaw. They regrouped, and, as with the Ghetto, they conquered the city block by block using heavy artillery to force people out, destroying every building in their path totally.

I remember seeing the heavy German Panzer with its big gun swiveling to point at the target. The gun was pointed down, shooting into the basements and bunkers where people had taken refuge or were hiding. The brutal Wlasow Army soldiers and SS regiments were catching people for use as human shields on the Eastern Front, or killing on the spot everyone who emerged. As the walls collapsed or fires started, people had no choice but to run into the street to be captured.

My parents both had cyanide capsules to take if needed. I remember seeing the capsules. They were reddish and, I thought, kind of big to be placed under the tongue, as my father directed. My father said there was no escape now; but my mother insisted that we could not give up, somebody had to survive and, she said, they (my parents) had to survive for the child. What would happen to me if they abandoned me? They had to fight to the end by whatever means became available: "Ja sie nie daje do tych cholernych bandytow, i moje dziecko nigdy im nie zostawie" (I will not be giving in to these cholera-like bandits, and my child I will never leave to them), she said with all her strength and passion. Then my father agreed. The moment passed. That was the only time I ever saw those tablets or heard them talk about suicide. But I know that they had them all along, and maybe I just didn't understand when I was younger. I was seven now; I had learned to read, and I understood everything. Using a chess board, my father had also taught me how to count, add, subtract, divide, and multiply; he even taught me the elements of chess, even though we did not have all the pieces.

. . .

During many of the metamorphoses, the personas of my adult life, I avoided as much as I could—such as exposure to books and movies about the Holocaust. I was afraid. I feared that it would initiate a search in me that I could never satisfy, like the real search that so many survivors were desperately caught up in after the war, looking and looking for lost children, parents, brothers, sisters, friends, or even just a trace of what happened to them, exactly where and how were they destroyed. My search, that I was so afraid of for so many years, would be truly frustrating and, I feared, paralyzing. It would be a search for lost memories, for reminders, for anything familiar that I recognized, that matched and added to one of those pictures I have in the incomplete gallery of my mind's eye. The fear I had of starting on this search was, I now believe, that once launched, it would take over my life to the exclusion of all else and would, of course, bring to the surface the long suppressed gallery of emotionally charged images, feelings and sounds that I devoted so much energy to keeping hidden below the surface of my consciousness. And, indeed, after sixty years, here I am writing this memoir and completely obsessed with it.

I was right. In the last two years, my daughter Simone and I have made two trips to Warsaw, and we are planning a third. Upon returning to our normal lives in California, we are inevitably asked: So, how was it? What did you do there? Oddly, questions very difficult to answer because what we were actually doing was doomed to failure and disappointment. We were searching for a lost world. The lamentable truth is that the cleansing of Poland is complete. The genocide was a success. What had been a vibrant culture in which my family had been deeply involved is gone forever. The people, too, are gone. There are very few traces of Jewish life in Poland left. Yet, at the outbreak of the Second World War in 1939, it was everywhere. There were more than three million Jews living in Poland, and about a third of Warsaw was Jewish, with an energetic cultural life known and respected throughout Europe. Today it is gone and cannot be found in Poland.

I am not sure what all the complex circumstances were that caused me to begin. But it was not long after I went to see The Pianist, an impeccably researched production in which I actually saw one of the images in my mind's gallery: a German Panzer tank with the big swivel gun that caused the remains of the building, including the bunker we were in, to collapse on top of us. I was crouching by a wall in what I thought was the safest place because I was under a picture of the Virgin Mary.

When my father died in 1969, the loss of him took so much from my being that I was no longer whole, and I knew I had to find help somehow, somewhere. My mother was also in great need, but though I was with her and went through the motions, I could not truly mourn with her because I was still in a persona, not truly myself. I think she knew and felt the loneliness, was bereft, but I was powerless to change myself in those circumstances, barely holding on, and not able to let go.

My parents lived in Toronto. I, too, lived in Toronto. I was then, and had been for many years, a television producer-director for the CBC. When my father died I was in New York working at NBC for the CBC: I was there with Patrick Watson. When I got the phone call from my mother, I knew immediately that I should not have gone off in pursuit of my fashionable and exciting career, leaving my father in the hospital and my mother alone to cope. It was wrong of me, and to this day I feel great guilt-ridden sorrow for my inability to express in my actions the love and attachment I felt for my mother and my father. I needed the distance from them that I had created in order to be the necessary persona for the particular metamorphosis of my life that I was living at the time. The alternative was to be the child of my parents; that was too dangerous. I could not sustain the anxiety, and still remain a functioning adult. But when my father died, I had to look for help.

At that time of my life, I was able to absorb and understand whole areas of life or study by immersion in the relevant literature. I read some psychology, quickly found Freud, and buried myself in psychoanalysis. Then I read R. D. Laing. It was not just that he was all the rage in that period; I was drawn to him because he opposed orthodoxy, approved of oddness and idiosyncrasy, and appeared to have a much quicker fix than psychoanalysis; and he was a Scotsman, just like Bill Thompson, my husband at that time. It all fit perfectly.

I went to London and made an avant-garde program about R. D. Laing in which Ronnie, a little drunk, dressed in a kurta, lying across his bed, with his gorgeous little curly-headed three-year-old son running about in the background, recited the poems from his next book, Knots. I loved my show and was proud of it and its originality. I had my new persona and it stabilized me. But I continued to search for myself, to immerse myself more and more in Freud and psychoanalysis. I had reached bottom too quickly with Laing. After Knots, there was silence, as Laing himself deteriorated and succumbed. I started to undergo Freudian analysis and began the never-ending task of my life: the search for myself. Four years into my analysis, I met Jeff Masson, then a Sanskrit scholar teaching at the University of Toronto and also passionately interested in Freud and psychoanalysis.

When Jeff and I met, married, and constructed our life together, I seemed well, sophisticated, with a wonderful career at the CBC. I seemed well; but I was not well. I was still not myself, still searching, and too vulnerable to loss. Nonetheless, Jeff was Jewish, ex nostris, and he seemed safe. I loved him and was ecstatically happy to be with a beautiful, exciting Jewish man and to have a child with him. My mother, too, was happy. Finally, we had a family. My issues remained unresolved; I hung on as long as I could, but eventually it all came crashing down.

That's another story. Now back to the really hard part. The war of all wars that I survived. As a small child, often by my wits, I survived a persecution that gave rise to the term genocide. As an adult, I paid the price; I was unwell.

. . .

And so, here I go, where I left off, back to the dark gallery in my mind's eye. Back to that bunker in the basement of a bombed-out building. One night when the bombs were whistling loud and clear and loud explosions sounded very close, I was crouching by a wall, as I had been told to do when the bombs were falling, when suddenly everything seemed to collapse in flying dust all around me. That taste of dust in my mouth and the loud noise is the last thing that I remember when the wall collapsed and I was buried.

My father was apparently nearby and frantically dug me out. I remember seeing the sky, light and silvery in the eerie light of the moon, ruins, and piles of rubble all around. I was bobbing up and down in my father's arms as he carried me quickly outside, saying, "Breathe, breathe deeply the good fresh air." Evidently, I came through that episode unscathed but for some scrapes and bruises that my father carefully examined and cleaned as well as he could. We had to stay hidden because there were soldiers and tanks everywhere.

I remember, after the episode when I was buried and dug up without much harm, much discussion in the bunker about how I had been saved and protected by the power of the Virgin Mary, Mother of God, because apparently there had been a medallion of the Virgin Mary hanging on the wall that had buried me. This led to much praying with rosaries by everyone all around me because I had been so blessed. My mother, as always, tried to blend in. My father stood apart, gaunt and alone.

CHAPTER 7

Escape

_____

I don't know how many days passed. But finally our turn came. What remained of the building we were in was ablaze and filled with smoke. We had to run out into the street and be shot or captured. We were captured. They were separating out the men. When they took my father, my mother begged and pleaded for him. No response. It seemed hopeless. My mother whispered to me: "We are lucky; these are young German soldiers who maybe will not hurt a child. Run to your father, scream, yell, cry, plead for them to let him stay with us." I understood immediately what I had to do. I hastened toward my father, crying hysterically; it caused me to run into the butt of the rifle the soldier was shifting to aim or to use to move my father away. As the collision occurred, I grabbed that wooden butt and hung on with all my strength, pulling and screaming at the top of my lungs, begging for my father to stay with me. I succeeded in creating such a fracas that the young *über lieutenant* in charge, unwilling to shoot a child, just as my mother predicted, had no choice but to let my father stay with us. My mother later said that he told her, as he gave the order, "It does not matter, one man more or less in front of the Panzers on the Russian front; his fate will be the same either way."

The crowd of women and children, now including me, my mother, and my father, all of those captured from the bombed-out buildings reduced to rubble that day, were then marched in the front of a Panzer tank, with its big gun aimed and soldiers with whips and guns on both sides, to an empty area, smaller than a football field. The only building in sight was like a makeshift barracks with a guard hut for the soldiers at the front, across the only road. The whole area was surrounded by barbed wire.

There was no food or water and all the younger children were expressing their hunger, fear, and misery. My mother went around to talk to everyone, saying that somehow we had to get out, to escape, or we would all be murdered very soon if we did not die of starvation first. My mother also surreptitiously observed, whenever she could, what was going on in the guard hut, who was on duty and when.

There was one soldier who looked younger and less arrogant than the others. Whenever this soldier was there by himself, my mother would go there and engage him in conversation in her beautiful German. She heard all about his life and family, his desire to marry and have children; he showed her pictures over which she exclaimed appropriately; she told him stories of her family, all Volksdeutsche, she said, and only held there by error, by a bureaucratic mishap that is especially so very unfortunate because the child (me) is frail and may never recover from this unfortunate mistake if we have to remain here without food and water much longer. As you can see, she said, tossing her red locks and looking at him sideways, I am a very trustworthy person and you can be sure that I will do everything in my power to make sure your superiors know that by your intelligent action this terrible error was corrected and that they commend you appropriately. All you need to do is let us leave and I will take care of the rest. I know this area well and I know where to get help from friendly German-speaking folks.

It was getting dark. My mother spent a few more minutes exclaiming over the young soldier's family photos, and quickly walked back to us, the soldier staring after her wide-eyed. "He won't shoot. Let's go quickly," she said, "before it occurs to him to speak with anyone. I think I have him confused now; let's go." My mother, my father and I then rapidly set off toward the guard hut, with my mother a little ahead, the soldier watching us, bewildered, as we approached.

In the meantime, other people decided to take the risk of walking out. A whole column of women and children had formed behind us and were keeping the rapid pace, past the guard hut with the bewildered young soldier still standing in the same spot, staring after the quickly moving column; all of us following my mother, all trying to disappear in a bend of the road. It seems that now we were walking, then running toward a tall wall, as if we were in a fort. Then, as if miraculously, strong men appeared, forming ladders against the wall with their hands and bodies, helping everyone up, over the wall, into the open farming country at the end of the field, beyond the wall. I remember being handed up one man's body to his shoulders, then to the top of the wall by a tree to make it easier to get down on the other side, using the branches to shorten the fall. My mother had gone first to help me. There were trees on the other side of the field. And we all ran as fast as possible for cover. In fact, this was an old fort, perhaps from medieval times, on the outskirts of Warsaw. The Germans were using it to contain some Russian prisoners of war and these were the men who came to our aid by helping us over the wall that night.

By this time, we could hear a machine gun firing and rifle shots resounding from the direction of the guard hut. I suppose our naïve young soldier had come to and called for help. We did not know if anyone fell. I barely remember the other people with us. I know that people dispersed. Only a small group remained together. I remember the others only vaguely. I suppose they were Poles and had nothing to fear in the Polish countryside. That was not the case for us. Every person we encountered could be a dangerous enemy who might betray us immediately. I knew this; I do not know how.

My mother and father agreed on a plan. We would walk east, toward the Russian front. We would walk at night and hide in any shelter we could find in the forest during the day. We had to avoid all people and watch out for military patrols, which were everywhere.

We walked for more than a month. My mother foraged for food, stealing from the fields whenever possible; she was not afraid of dogs and sometimes brought eggs from a chicken coop; she could often steal beets or whatever from storage containers or barrels, things like pickles and cucumbers. My father taught me how to eat eggs raw. He insisted I eat them, but I hated them even then. My father also knew about wild roots and leaves, and we ate those. But the winter was coming and it was getting very cold.

Then one night we found an abandoned house in the forest. We pushed inside, looking for warmth. There was a staircase and I ran up to look out. I wanted to be the all-important lookout. There was a window and I ran to it, but before I could even look around, I heard someone shout what I thought was, "Uwaga, niemcy ida" (Beware, the Germans are coming), and with terror in my gut I jumped out of the window.

The next thing I remember is my father's face leaning over me. He was holding my left wrist very tightly to stop the bleeding; there was blood everywhere. I had fallen on a broken bottle and nearly severed the artery. My father closed the wound with a safety pin and bound it tightly to prevent bleeding. It turned out it was a false alarm; the patrol had not seen the house and had passed. But at this point, my parents agreed that we could not survive the winter nights in the forest and that we would have to find shelter with probably hostile peasants.

My mother went ahead to see what she could discover in the next village. My father thought we were close to the eastern border of Poland, close to the Russian front. My mother was gone for what seemed like an eternity. She came back the next night and said she had found a place. One of the wealthier peasants in the village was an old woman. She and her two grown sons were epileptics. She would shelter us in her hut and feed us in return for my father's medical services for their affliction. I remember that my father explained that he could not cure them but that he could teach them what to do to make their seizures more predictable and less dangerous. He told them stories about all the great men who had been epileptic, how they followed in an illustrious tradition, and how it was an illness not to be ashamed of. They could learn from it how best to live with it. My mother, I could see, was worried, but his gentle candor worked, and after that they received us with open arms. Of course, they did not know we were Jews. That would have been too dangerous to reveal. If they suspected, they did not say. The subject remained taboo.

I was the child of the household, and to show respect to my father I was given the place of honor to sleep, the warmest place in the now very severe winter, the old woman's bed under her huge eiderdown. I was warm every night, but I stayed awake as much as I could because I was terrified of getting accidentally strangled or squashed to death if the big old woman had an epileptic attack. I had seen her and one of her sons have a seizure shortly after we had first come, and it had filled me with dread. But, I also knew and really understood that we depended on this woman for our lives: she gave us shelter. We could not offend her sensibility. So every night I did what I had to do and said nothing.

I spent all my time in the hut, drawing on the frozen window, except for quick outings to the outhouse in the frozen air that seemed so cold that it was not breathable. There was a thick undulating cover of snow wherever you looked. It snowed often with large, soft flakes. When it stopped snowing a very cold wind blew, and it seemed even colder then. The villagers did not socialize in the winter. I suppose there must have been a church for Sunday Mass, but I do not remember. I had to stay inside, in order not to attract attention and get people asking questions. That would be dangerous.

One day, as the winter lost its most icy cold, we heard a rumbling noise, gathering magnitude, that seemed to be coming from the road. The road spoke before we saw anything. My mother ran out, put her ear to the ground and cried out,

"It's either the Wlasow, and we are finished, or it's the Russian front, and we will live! But the roar is an army on the march." I ran to her to hear what she heard, but she told me to go in the hut and hide until we knew for sure. Very soon, as the first soldiers appeared, my mother ran up to them to see the insignia on their hats. If it was the red star, it was the Russian army, and they were friends not foes. When she saw the red star, she was overjoyed and began dancing and singing in the street in front of the advancing front line.

CHAPTER 8

Return

_____

This summer, Simone and I went to Poland again, the second year in a row, still searching in vain for traces of my lost family and ancestry that had been so much a part of life in Poland before 1939. This time we actually drove to Golub Dobrzyn where my grandfather's estate had been, and where I was born.

We tried to talk to an old man who reputedly knew the whole history of the region, but he was so hostile; he refused to say anything and the whole environment felt dangerous, cold, and totally uninterested in regret for things past. I could not forget that this was pogrom country after all, where murder had occurred, even after that terrible war, and where hatred of Jews was so deep that anything was possible. Why was this racism so stubborn that it could even outlive genocide? Simone and I, after the sad and weighty discomfort of these encounters, quickly returned to Warsaw, to the comfort and safety of our hotel.

Still, I am not satisfied, I need to continue the search for that lost world and we are planning another trip next year. I think this is because I truly have a dilemma. Warsaw feels like home to me, and in a haunting way I love that city so beloved of my mother, who loved to sing it love songs. Yet, just below the surface of that civil, polite life lurk the murderous horrors of the past, and I feel that

I have betrayed my family by participating with pleasure in the use of the language and engaging with that lying civility. Where is Yiddish, that beautiful, soft language, and all those who spoke it and lived life in these streets? Often in Warsaw I feel I should run through the city crying out that this question has no answer, that they have gone to dust, never to return. Poland has been cleansed. "There Once Was a World" that is no more, but I am a remnant of that world, "And I Still See Their Faces,"[1] and I hear the dying lament of that world that was to be my world.

· · ·

In Warsaw this summer, August 2005, Simone and I located a second or third cousin, Magda Kurowska, ten years older than me, whose mother was Fela Rosenbaum, who perished in Birkenau in 1943. This is her story.

Magda's mother, Fela, was a very beautiful and accomplished young woman from the wealthy Rosenbaum family. The Rosenbaums and the Alters, my father's family, were related, came from Radomsko, and had lands and estates in Pławno, near Radomsko. Fela was brought up there, was an accomplished horsewoman, and fell in love with a Polish cavalry officer. This was before the war. They married and had a daughter, Magda.

As a child and adolescent, Magda spent much time in beautiful Pławno with her mother and her grandmother whom she loved very much. Both her grandparents died in 1936. But she continued to spend time in Pławno with her mother.

1   This is a reference to the title of the book by Gołda Tencer and the Shalom Foundation, *And I Still See Their Faces: Images of Polish Jews* (Warsaw: American-Polish-Israeli SHALOM Foundation, 1998).

The person she remembers vividly from those happy days is someone she called Ciocia Alter (meaning Auntie Alter). It turns out that Ciocia Alter was Salomea Alter, my father's mother, my grandmother. The fact is that our grandmothers, Magda's and mine, were sisters, and we remembered my grandmother, her Auntie Alter, the same way. A tall, slim woman with a long oval face, sad eyes, and wearing long earrings accentuating her long face.

Magda also remembered my father. "Doktor Alter," she said, "of course I knew him, and his wife Hanka; they had a daughter, you know; I wonder what happened to her?" "Magda, Magda, *kochana* (dear), look at me. That's me. I am the daughter of Hanka and Elek Alter."

"Oh," she said, embracing me warmly. "We are really very closely related." We were both happy for a moment. Then she said, "You know, I see my mother's face so often." The sadness enveloped us again and she told me the whole story.

Epilogue
Life after the War

January, 1946. At age eight, we leave Poland forever and temporarily settle in France. Both my mother and father had studied in Liège, Belgium, prewar and both were French-speaking.

1949. At age eleven to twelve, my mother and I cross the Atlantic to New York aboard the *Queen Mary* to visit cousins living there since before the war. I had totally adapted to France, I loved France; both my mother and I disliked the USA and after a few months we returned to France. One of the cousins, though, a dentist named Henry, Uncle Henry, was a sailor. He had a boat in New Rochelle and sailed the Long Island Sound every weekend. He taught this little survivor of the Ghetto how to sail, how to swim, and how to love the ocean. I retained these lessons and inclinations for the rest of my life. To this day, I love the beach and the ocean—a warm calm ocean like the sound in the summer, most of all.

1951. After much debate and argument (my mother wanted to remain in a civilized country, in Europe, my father wanted to go to a wilderness with no people), my father won the argument and we all emigrated to Canada, to Saskatoon in the west, where as a physician my father would eventually obtain a license to practice medicine, after four years of service as a chest surgeon in a tuberculosis sanatorium. I hated life in Canada with a passion; there was antisemitism just under the surface of that orderly, religious, mediocre life.

Shortly thereafter, at age fourteen, I go away on my own to the University of Manitoba in Winnipeg to be a student in the Faculty of Fine Arts.

1954–1960. I study general sciences at the University of Toronto, and English literature at Western, in London, Ontario; I live in a commune of British medical and doctoral biochemistry students and become a high school history teacher in the Canadian north.

1960s. I become a news writer for the just-opened TV station in London, Ontario. I write all the news and voice-overs for the two local news broadcasts and edit all the footage; in 1962, I become the writer and producer-director of documentary programs as well.

I marry my first husband, Bill Thompson, one of the bio-chemists from the commune, and become Terri Thompson.

We move to England where I work for the BBC as a writer and for the British Council as a translator.

We return to Toronto and I work as a producer-director in public affairs for the CBC. In that capacity, I write all of my own shows and put out about two hundred programs a year for the next decade or so.

I also develop a strong interest in live theatre, and direct a production at Toronto's famed Royal Alexandra Theatre of three short Canadian plays by working playwrights.

Bill and I divorce.

1970s. I meet Jeff Masson; and in 1971, Jeff and I marry and I become Terri Masson.

I continue part-time at the CBC and study in the philosophy Department at Toronto's York University. I attend graduate school at the University of Toronto and become a lecturer at York in philosophy.

I have a keen interest in psychoanalysis and I undergo traditional Freudian analysis. Jeff and I share this interest, and he applies to the Toronto Psychoanalytic Institute to become an analyst. We write papers together that are published in the *International Journal of Psychoanalysis* and given by Jeff at the meeting of the International Psychoanalytical Association in Paris.

In 1974, our daughter Simone is born.

In 1979, we move to Berkeley, California, and I start a new career as a headhunter for the burgeoning computer chip industry in Silicon Valley.

1980s. Jeff and I separate and then divorce in 1982.

I meet a woman, Deborah Kenoyer, with whom I will share the rest of my life.

I go to law school in San Francisco, while working as a taxi driver. I graduate at the age of fifty-two, pass the bar, and begin a new career as a lawyer.

I am forced to withdraw from the state Bar because of a gambling problem that I am unable to control for many years.

1990s. I become a legal consultant to a large transportation company in the Bay area, and then work as a consultant in a variety of different capacities.

2002. I suffer a brain aneurysm that requires surgery. This is a debilitating injury, but I manage to recover, almost to my full capacity, over the next several years, and I continue to work as a consultant.

2004–2005. Simone and I take our first trips to Warsaw, and I begin writing my memoir.

Photo Gallery

Figure 1. Young Hanka Fuleder, Terri's mother, with her mother, Roza Ripin-Fuleder.

Figure 2. Young Hanka (right) with her sisters Erna (Esther; middle front), Ruth (left), and their tutor (middle back).

Figure 3. Young Hanka (right) and her sister Erna (Esther; left).

Figure 4. Terri's maternal grandfather, Joseph Fuleder.

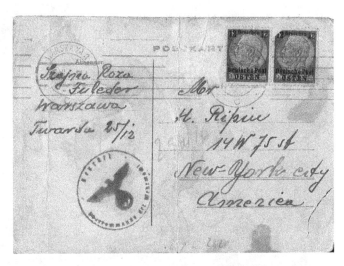

Figure 5. Postcard from Warsaw Ghetto, 1940, address side.

24/6 1940
Lieber Bruder. Nach so fielen schrei-
-ben durch "Hajas" und durch "Joint",
sind wir ohne nachricht fou euch,
Sorgt Ihr was für uns? wir sind
in sehr eine kritische lage, wir
haben nicht kein mittel zum
leben. helft uns schnel wie
meglich erwarte baldige antwort
besten Grüsse und küsse wie
von uns alle deine liebende
schwester Roza

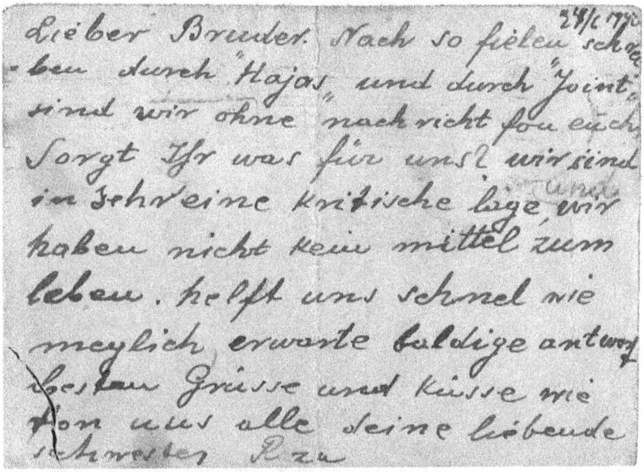

Figure 6. Postcard from Warsaw Ghetto, 1940.

Figure 7. Terri's parents, Hanka and Elek, standing by Powązki cemetery wall. Photographed by Uncle Marek Rozenbaum-Majewski.

Figure 8. Elek and Halina Gebasz.

Figure 9. Hanka and Halina Gebasz.

Figure 10. Halina Gebasz with Terri wearing the uniform of the Polish Scouts.

Figure 11. Hanka and Elek, date unknown.

Figure 12. Terri with her parents, immediately postwar.

Figure 13. Whole group postwar.

Figure 14. Terri and her mother, postwar.

Figure 15. Little Terri standing on railing in front of the Kutno home.

Figure 16. Elek Alter ID cards.

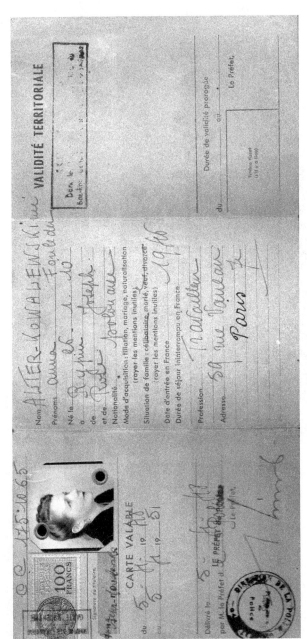

Figure 17. Hanka French travel card.

Figure 18. Terri and her mother in France, postwar.

Figure 19. Uncle Marek Rozenbaum-Majewski.

Figure 20. Hanka and Elek in Canada.

Figure 21. Terri, c. 1950s.

Figure 22. Terri on her wedding day, 1971.

Figure 23. Terri c. 1980s.

Figure 24. Terri and her mother in Berkeley, CA, 1980s.

Figure 25. Terri with her newly obtained birth certificate, 2006.

Figure 26. Terri in front of the Kutno home, 2006.

Figure 27. Terri visiting Hotel Jeanne D'arc, in Paris 2014. She lived there with her family after arriving in Paris in 1946.

Figure 28. Terri in Warsaw, 2014, by the Monument of the Fighters and the Martyrs.

Figure 29. Terri with her cousin, Magda Kurowska, in Warsaw, 2014.

Figure 30. Terri in Treblinka, 2014.

Figure 31. Terri (middle) with Simone (left) and Elżbieta (right) walking in Treblinka, 2014.

Figure 32. Terri, Simone, and Elzbieta at Treblinka camp, 2014.

Afterword

Her Kaddish: Contextualizing Thérèse C. Masson's *My Kaddish: A Child Speaks from the Warsaw Ghetto*

———

If not for the Greater German Reich, the Holocaust would not have happened—at least, not then and not that way. *My Kaddish: A Child Speaks from the Warsaw Ghetto,* by Thérèse C. Masson (née Klara Alter), pertains to the Holocaust of Poland's Jews in which the Polish context played an important and more often than not decisive role as its framework. From this comes the idea of providing the text with the local context even though it is but one of the dimensions of this double testimony about the fight for survival and the subsequent fight for surviving one's own survival.

The Warsaw Ghetto

Klara Alter was born in 1937 in Golub-Dobrzyń to a large Jewish family with two main branches: the Alters and the Fuleders. As a consequence of the outbreak of WWII, the Fuleders' real estate—including a family house in Kutno that survived WWII—found itself in the part of Poland that was directly annexed to the Third Reich as the Reichsgau Wartheland. The annexation was followed by spoliation and a forced resettlement of the non-German populations. The property of the Alters, in turn, found itself in the occupied part of the country that was transformed into the so-called Generalgouvernement (GG). The spoliation policy there targeted Jews almost exclusively.

The Fuleders and the Alters, the maternal and paternal families of Thérèse C. Masson, became inmates of the Warsaw Ghetto. As opposed to the majority of the six hundred ghettos established in occupied Poland by the Germans, the Warsaw Ghetto was closed and walled. It was created on November 15, 1940, after more than one year of Polish antisemitic violence ravaging the streets of Warsaw with Jews frequently beaten and Jewish shops robbed in broad daylight. The period in question was also marked by the week-long Warsaw pogrom at Easter, 1940. Avoiding the ghetto, especially as a large family, was impossible because of the informal Polish supervision of the ghettoization process. Twelve thousand people (as many as fell victim to the Vél' d'Hiv' Roundup in occupied Paris in 1942) were forced into the Warsaw Ghetto by the Polish blue police based on personal denunciations. While having a Jewish background, many of them were of Christian denominations and didn't even consider themselves Jewish. Their neighbors, Poles of Christian descent, decided for them.

Cut off from their savings, property, and the possibility of practicing their professions, ghetto inmates lived mostly from underselling to Poles what they still possessed. The subsistence of Klara Alter's family was additionally secured by at least two working male family members: Klara's father, Eljasz Alter (1905–1969), was allowed to practice as a physician[1] and Klara's paternal uncle joined the Jewish Service of Order (Jüdischer Ordnungsdienst).

While registering in the "list of physicians non-Aryans," Eljasz Alter declared his address to be 29 Ogrodowa Street[2] (the building survived WWII); Klara's maternal grandparents, the Fuleders (Roza Szajna née Ripin and Josef), lived at 25 Twarda Street, apartment 12. The latter address may be found on a postcard that was sent by Klara's maternal grandmother Roza Szajna to a brother in New York City in June 1940 with a request for help. Ogrodowa and Twarda Streets belonged to two different parts of the Warsaw Ghetto: the so-called "large ghetto" and "small ghetto." They were separated by an "Aryan" street that during the first half of 1942 was spanned by one of the ghetto's wooden footbridges. Otherwise, passersby had to endure sophisticated humiliations at the hands of the German gendarmerie at the ground crossing of the internal border strip.

Before 1942

Before the author's world ultimately disintegrated, its integrity didn't cease to be put at risk. The first such moment seems to be the disappearance of her father. We don't know under what pretext Eljasz Alter was incarcerated at the Pawiak prison. Located deep in the large ghetto, Pawiak had been

---

1   Cf. Lista lekarzy nie-aryjczyków [A list of physicians non-Aryans], in Maria Ciesielska, *Lekarze getta warszawskiego* [Physicians of the Warsaw ghetto] (Warszawa: Wydawnictwo Dwa Światy, 2017), 290, 314–315.
2   Ibid., 314.

transformed by the German authorities into the central custody site for both the ghetto inmates and the "Aryan side" dwellers. The most common Jewish "crime" punishable by death was crossing the ghetto walls. However "illegal," going outside the Warsaw Ghetto was not physically impossible. It often ended badly because Poles reported Jews to the Polish police or German authorities. As Israel Gutman, a Warsaw-born survivor and historian, put it: "Around that wall there was another wall"[3]—a wall made of the Polish majority's attitudes and behaviors that had the effect of sealing the interstices of the wall made of bricks. Eljasz Alter could also have been taken hostage as a result of the German predilection for collective responsibility for the "crimes" the German authorities ceaselessly multiplied with their "legal" ingenuity.

In a research study on the Pawiak prison Janina Gruszkowa wrote: "Whereas the SS attitude to Poles was cruel, if subject to fluctuations; their attitude to Jews was devoid of any human feature."[4] Pawiak was (in)famous for its torture—beatings and "physical exercises"—that many prisoners were unable to survive. Eljasz Alter doesn't seem to be on the prison files, commonly the case with those among Jewish prisoners who were destined to be killed. Eventually, he was ripped out of Pawiak thanks to an operation orchestrated by his brother and, certainly, with substantial bribery. As Terri testifies in her

---

3   Prof. Israel Gutman interviewed by Barbara Engelking, *Zagłada Żydów*, no. 9 (2013): 226.

4   Janina Gruszkowa, *Pawiak—więzienie Gestapo w Warszawie* [Pawiak—the Gestapo prison in Warsaw], in *Biuletyn Głównej Komisji Badania Zbrodni Niemieckich w Polsce*, vol. 4 (Warszawa: Wydawnictwo Głównej Komisji Badania Zbrodni Niemieckich w Polsce, 1948), 24.

memoir, after three days of imprisonment "His body was broken for evermore."

In the years 1940–1942, nearly one hundred thousand Warsaw Ghetto inmates died from starvation, disease, and cold, which, in part, occurred on the ghetto streets. Klara was on these streets and remembered the details. Time after time, the danger and the pain reached her body and mind, but they still could have been perceived by her as external. She was still surrounded by her parents and her maternal and paternal grandparents, as well as numerous aunts and uncles. Even while suffering from starvation and diseases, "because of the corpses and the rats," she was protected as much as possible from the ghetto reality.

This protection was possible until the Grossaktion Warschau of the summer 1942, that is, the deportation of some three hundred thousand ghetto inmates to the gas chambers at the nearby Treblinka death camp. The massacre was part of the Aktion Reinhardt, the mass industrial killing of the Jews of the Generalgouvernement and Bezirk Bialystok by the Germans and their helpers. It cost the lives of 1,700,000 of Poland's Jews. The Grossaktion Warschau lasted from July 22 until September 21, 1942. Subsequently, the Warsaw Ghetto was reduced to six labor camps, with thirty-five thousand "legal" Jewish workers who hid and supported around twenty-five thousand "illegal" relatives.

Klara's memories from the ghetto encompass the experience of hiding *intra muros* that corresponds to the Grossaktion exactly. Earlier, ghetto inmates had been allowed to move around within the ghetto limits without having to justify their existence. At the hour of the deportation, the medical doctors as well as the members of the Ordnungsdienst were declared to be allowed to remain alive together with their close ones—at first. Then came the hour of the Kettle (*kocioł*).

The Kettle

The Warsaw Umsiedlungsaktion or Grossaktion started—as already said—on July 22, 1942, after the ghetto had been surrounded by Lithuanians, Latvians, and the Polish police. At the very beginning, the ghetto's prisoners were taken to the Umschlagplatz from their places of residence. After about one week, the procedure was taken over by the Germans and their Ukrainian assistants, as the Jewish Service of Order, initially forced by the Germans to conduct the roundup, didn't execute the German orders rigorously enough. Then, still in the first half of August, selection started being conducted directly at the Umschlagplatz, where everyone had to assemble. It is not impossible, however, that Terri—the American transformation of Klara's occupation name "Teresa" that after the war, in France, became "Thérèse"—refers to the fourth stage of the Grossaktion: the Kettle. It is not impossible, since the families Fuleder and Alter were deported at that time; even though, given their social capital and material status, they most probably had been equipped with the necessary authorizations to stay temporarily alive. Moreover, Terri uses the term "Great Selection" and mentions an additional, specific order. This order was promulgated on September 5, 1942, after seven weeks of continuous mass deportations of Warsaw's Jews to the gas chambers at Treblinka II.

The so-called Great Selection or Great Reduction—a selection within a selection, a reduction within a reduction—was targeted precisely against those who had been previously authorized to stay alive together with their families: slave laborers, physicians and nurses, functionaries of the Jewish Council and its institutions, as well as the Jewish Service of Order. It was conducted at several checkpoints improvised in different places around the Umschlagplatz. The picture Terri remembered—the heat, the crowd, the deadly fear, people being shot, parents striving to smuggle their children out or abandoning them—couldn't be more accurate. In the face of deportations it often enough happened that ghetto prisoners killed their beloved ones and took their own lives. During the Great Reduction, female doctors from the children's hospital poisoned the babies they had under their care and gave morphine to the older children in order to prevent them from being conscious when they were shot in their beds by the Germans and their Ukrainian, Lithuanian, and Latvian accomplices.

Roza Szajna Ripin-Fuleder, Klara's maternal grandmother, was likely among the 2,648 people shot dead during the *kocioł*. Sixty others committed suicide. Some 339 died a so-called natural death due to the inhumane conditions of detention, more often than not in the open air, in the city block delimited by Smocza, Gęsia, Zamenhoffa, Szczęśliwa Streets and Parysowski Square. The number of ghetto inmates deported to Treblinka was 54,269. All that during the five days of the Kettle alone.

The Kettle occurred between September 6 and September 11, 1942. That year, Yom Kippur fell on September 21. This is when the Germans decided to end the Warsaw Umsiedlungsaktion

by executing the vast majority (2,020 out of 2,400) of the functionaries of the Jewish Service of Order. The Kettle fell between
Leil Selichot and Erev Rosh Hashana leading up to the High
Holidays. This is probably why Klara associated the described
events with Yom Kippur.

The "Aryan side"

After the Grossaktion Warschau, the Alters, reduced to three,
crossed to the "Aryan side." They did it in extremis thanks to
the determination, resourcefulness, and bravado of Klara's
mother, Anna Fuleder-Alter (1910–1996), and were occasionally assisted by her Polish friend Halina Gebasz, a Polish
Socialist Party (Polska Partia Socjalistyczna, PPS) member
and, just as importantly, an atheist. As was often the case of dis-
creet and subtle women, seemingly distant from the hardships
of everyday life, Klara's mother, known as Hanka, became the
indefatigable driving force behind the family's fight for survival on the "Aryan side." In a situation with no escape, she was
the parent who energetically rejected the prospect of suicide
and remained steadfast in her belief that the only way was "to
fight to the end by whatever means becomes available."

Once outside the ghetto walls, however, Klara herself had
to fight in what her peer Henryk Grynberg called a "Jewish
war for survival, in a permanent withdrawal."[5] Terri Masson
called it "our war." To set out on such a war at all required
money, connections, an appearance that cannot be detected as

---

5   Henryk Grynberg, *Obowiązek* [A duty], in *Monolog polsko-żydowski* [Polish Jewish monologue] (Wołowiec: Czarne, 2012), 105.

"resembling" (*podobny*)[6] or "recognizable" (*rozpoznawalny*)[7] by the vigilant Christian eye. To pass required cultural and linguistic skills (not speaking Polish "too badly" nor "too well," according to the vigilant Christian ear), the mental strength to maintain the act, physical stamina, nerves of steel, and suicidal bravery. All that was necessary, but not sufficient. The "Aryan side" was a human—or rather inhuman—minefield where every step could be the last. Chance decided. And chance had a Polish face.

Poles "arbitrated." In the "Jewish war" they were the effective "second instance" (that is, a kind of an "appellate body)." Around three hundred thousand Jews who fought for survival on the "Aryan side" lost their case "on appeal." The majority of the majority approved the German exterminatory endeavor, supplementing it with the lack of any alternative: robbing Jews systematically, hounding them from hideout to hideout,

---

6   "Resembling" (*podobny*) or "resembling the Jew" (*podobny do Żyda*)—as in the popular phrase, "a human being resembling the Jew" (*człowiek podobny do Żyda*)—refers to the practice of non-Jews scrutinizing people, with heightened attention and down to the tiniest detail, to identify traits that fit the antisemitic stereotype they nourished.

7   "To recognize" in wartime Polish didn't mean "to identify somebody from having encountered them before," but "to identify somebody as Jewish." "Recognizing" those who struggled to survive on the "Aryan side" was a murderous antisemitic social ritual, practiced individually and collectively, for money and in a "disinterested" way. Those who did it for money, jewelry, or other valuables were called *szmalcownicy*. *Szmalcownictwo* constituted an informal, but popular and lucrative, wartime profession. The blackmail consisted in the alternative: money or death (by means of handing over to the Polish police or the German authorities). Both forms of "recognition," whether "disinterested" or for money, constituted a lethal danger to the victims. The former triggered the latter. Stripping Jews of money, jewelry, or other valuables was not a minor crime. It meant depriving them of any chance of survival.

giving them away, and also killing them, without the knowledge of the German authorities. Poles had the power of life and death over those who managed to avoid extermination at the hands of the Germans. This is why they are remembered by their Jewish victims as "so-called compatriots," who, as a rule, turned out to be worse than the Germans.

Going outside to the "Aryan side" was a last resort because the "Aryan side" was not actually an outside. Jan Karski's statement—"The whole of Poland was a ghetto"[8]—captures how the whole of occupied Poland was a panoptic reality, a sociocultural apparatus that enabled permanent scrutiny and immediate identification, and guaranteed that even the smallest and most peripheral element was not overlooked. This was an apparatus that reached everywhere and everything and had neither exterior nor gap.[9] The omnipresent and all-seeing Christian observer "transformed the whole social body into a field of perception" with "thousands of eyes posted everywhere, mobile attentions ever on the alert"—with a particularly mighty role played by children.[10]

As Terri testifies: "Every person we encountered could be a dangerous enemy who might betray us immediately. I knew this; I do not know how." As a result, between thirty thousand and fifty thousand Jews, barely, managed to see out the war in occupied Poland. They survived mainly in German labor camps, German concentration camps, or partisan units in the

---

8 Jan Karski, *Widziałem* [I saw,] written down by Michał Cichy, *Gazeta Wyborcza*, October 2–3, 1999, 15.

9 Michel Foucault, *Discipline and Punish: The Birth of the Prison*, trans. A Sheridan London: Penguin, 1977), 228.

10 Ibid., 214.

forests in areas where Soviet partisans operated at the same time. Those who survived, like the Alters, with the occasional aid of non-Jews, constitute a tiny minority of this minority. Their total number is within the realm of statistical error.

The "Jewish War"

Fighting for survival on the "Aryan side" meant living in a panoptic reality, and a disciplinary society, on guard day and night, constantly on the run. Instructed by her mother, yet for quite some time deprived of the direct protection of her parents, Klara—now Teresa—had to fight for survival mostly on her own. Before she set out for her "Jewish war" as a five-year-old girl, her mother gave her two commandments: never look afraid and never look back. These words were to be understood literally, yet at the same time were heavily charged with a figurative meaning. As a consequence, her feelings had to be denied or blocked from her conscious self and her memories obliterated, which required putting shattering pressure on herself: "I suppressed my childish longing to be a child and learnt the skills of survival."

The transgression of the commandments meant immediate death. After the experience of living in the Warsaw Ghetto, Teresa could not understand any better what immediate death meant. She didn't need to grasp it with her mind. To use her term, it had been "ingrained" in her body. She saw her paternal grandparents (Salomea née Rozenbaum and Zelman Alter), as well as aunts and uncles, heading for the death trains; she saw her maternal grandfather being taken away in the same direction; she was at the shooting of her maternal grandmother.

She might not have realized what her grandmother's murder meant exactly, if not for the fact that at the very moment of the shooting she was held body-to-body by her mother. The child's body was communicated to by the mother's body more than the mother's entire being could bear and more than the child's entire being could bear—ever—together with an absurd but no less overwhelming feeling of guilt. As in the logic of a "choiceless choice" described by Lawrence L. Langer,[11] had the mother not "chosen" to save her daughter, perhaps she could have tried to save her own mother instead.

The second bodily communication—transmission and amplification—of mortal terror came from her father during what Eljasz Alter thought to be his final parting from his daughter. The source of danger and torment ceased to be exclusively external: "The horror of it became part of my body. [...] These are the deep lessons of my childhood that form the actual substance of my person, like bone and muscle form the body. To remove them is impossible without surgery."

Later came the psychological and physical tortures of hiding. Corporal punishment was meted out for Teresa's inability to contain her feelings. Seeing her female tormentor regularly rewarded with money and jewelry must have added yet another dimension to the challenge of self-suppression.

11 The scholar addresses "a crisis of what might call 'choiceless choice,' where critical decisions did not reflect options between life and death, but between one form of 'abnormal' response and another, both imposed by a situation that was in no way of the victim's own choosing" (Lawrence L. Langer, *The Dilemma of Choice in the Deathcamps*, *Centerpoint*, no. 5 [1980]: 224).

Further, the execution of Teresa's beloved rabbit must be mentioned. It happened on a farm where she tried to blend in; but instead of acceptance, she was singled out and bullied by the local children, suspicious of her being Jewish. It is not the children, however, but—once again—the amply remunerated adults in charge of the children who killed the animal. They did it with premeditation in order to make out of it a dish that they ostentatiously dedicated to Teresa. A kind of a murder by replacement and, in case she survived, a sure way to hurt her forever.

The Polish Context—Before the War

My Kaddish: A Child Speaks from the Warsaw Ghetto is a source for the history of the Holocaust in general. At the same time, it contributes to the history of a particular formation: the Polish Jewish intelligentsia that, despite its merit and countless proofs of its devotion to the country, was never accepted as a part of the nation proper. Scholarly literature refers to this demographic as a third nation,[12] and with more detailed contextualization locates its fate on a continuum of antisemitic violence, that is, a long-term process of elimination of Jews from Poland.

---

12 Cf. Anna Landau-Czajka, *"Syn będzie Lech" . . . Asymilacja Żydów w Polsce międzywojennej* ["Your son will be Lech" . . . Assimilation of Jews in interwar Poland] (Warszawa: Neriton, 2006); Helena Datner, *Ta i tamta strona. Żydowska inteligencja Warszawy drugiej połowy XIX wieku* [This and that side. The Jewish intelligentsia of Warsaw in the second half of the nineteenth century] (Warszawa: ŻIH, 2007).

And so, Klara Alter was born during the last year of a series of pogroms that wreaked havoc across Poland from 1935 to 1937. She was born the year the state instituted ghetto benches in Polish universities; the year *shechita* (kosher slaughter) was banned; the year in which the statute of the Association of Physicians of the Polish State (Związek Lekarzy Państwa Polskiego, ZLPP) was supplemented with the "Aryan paragraph." All of these were part and parcel of a bottom-up and top-down process of denying Jews the right to live in Poland, which did not suddenly begin in the 1930s.

The interwar Polish state that emerged after WWI was "inaugurated" with the pogroms of 1918–1919. The latter were preceded by anti-Jewish violence and followed by the pogroms of 1920, the internment of Jewish officers who volunteered for the Polish-Soviet War the same year, and the 1922 murder of the first Polish president, hunted down and shot dead as a "Jewish king". The Doctrine of the Polish Majority, which excluded Jews from the government of the state, at the price of violating the constitution, was adopted across the political spectrum from the left to the right (except for Jewish parties and the parties who were absent from the Polish parliament such as the communists). Like other East European countries established after WWI, Poland was forced at Versailles in 1918 to secure the citizenship and rights of minorities, but in fact never intended to honor this, and unilaterally withdrew from the Little Treaty of Versailles in 1934.

Prewar eliminationist political programs and the antisemitic policies of the Polish state were accompanied by exterminatory fantasies and slogans like "Death to Jews!" that could be heard on countless occasions—for example, during the student riots in Warsaw in 1937, the year Klara was born.[13] However, antisemitic violence at universities was not confined to the 1930s. Both Klara's parents went to study abroad in the French-speaking Belgian city of Liège in the 1920s. They might have decided to do so to avoid the antisemitic restrictions of the *numerus clausus* and the risk of physical harm by the Polish Christian male students armed with clubs topped off with razors, or the female students using naked fists and nails. The leading razor squads (*żyletkarze*) came from the faculties of law and medicine. Eljasz Alter, a dedicated pacifist, graduated as a medical doctor in 1931 from Liège university. Terri Masson would repeat that her father stopped being a patriot once he understood what it meant. And she went on to declare herself in one of the languages that were her own: "Je ne suis patriote d'aucun pays."

Synergy

In 1938, as Klara turned one, the Polish parliament passed and the Polish president signed a law which allowed the state to withdraw citizenship from any citizen who "was active abroad to the detriment of the Polish state or who was living abroad continuously for a period of at least five years after the [1918—E. J.] establishment of the Polish State, and who

---

13 Cf. Ludwik Krzywicki, *Ekscesy antyżydowskie na polskich uczelniach w latach trzydziestych XX w.* [Anti-Jewish excesses at Polish universities in the 1930] (Warszawa: Towarzystwo Wydawnicze i Literackie, 2009), 113–114.

had lost contact with the Polish State."[14] From the consular instructions, it became apparent that the purpose of the law was to cut off the return route to Poland for Polish Jews residing in Germany and Austria (approximately seventy thousand people.) Their impending influx had been expected as a result of the intensification of Nazi persecution policies. When the Polish consular offices announced passport controls for Polish citizens, the Third Reich decided on the policy of enforced faits accomplis. In an action organized by Reinhard Heydrich with Heinrich Himmler's approval, thousands of Jewish citizens of Poland who had been robbed of their possessions by the German Nazi state were taken to the German-Polish border and driven by bayonets into Poland.

In Poland, the majority of them were blocked from proceeding any further into the country. The border town of Zbąszyń was transformed into an internment camp for roughly seventeen thousand Jewish citizens of Poland. Soon afterwards, the situation became a humanitarian catastrophe. On November 7, 1938, under the influence of news from Zbąszyń, the Polish citizen Herszel Grynszpan shot the Nazi diplomat Ernst vom Rath in Paris. This event was used by the Third Reich as "grounds" for Kristallnacht—a series of pogroms, arrests, and property destruction organized and coordinated by the Nazi leadership, which ravaged Germany on the night of November 9 to 10, 1938. The year 1939, in turn, was intended by the Polish authorities to be the year of

---

14 Law of March 31, 1938—concerning deprivation of citizenship (*Journal of Laws*, no. 22, position 91).

questioning the Polish citizenship of all Jewish inhabitants of Poland.

Given that there was almost no way to leave Poland, was denying Jews the right to live in Poland radically different from denying them the right to live at all? In any case, mentally, emotionally, and at the level of social practices, Polish dominant culture and the majority of Polish society entered smoothly into a relationship of synergy with Nazi antisemitic policies. As a little girl, Klara had to confront that synergy.

The Polish role in the Holocaust is to be apprehended in the prewar to postwar continuum of antisemitic violence in the country as its middle wartime link. Instead of being perpetrated "on the margins of the Holocaust," as some historians would assert, Polish antisemitic violence constituted the framework of the Holocaust process. The term "collaboration," however, is not quite accurate when applied to the country. Poland belonged to the anti-Nazi alliance, and even though there was collaboration on the part of the former Polish state police, there was no collaborationist government. The hardships of the German Nazi occupation inflicted upon the non-Jewish population were considerable, as was the Polish hatred of the Germans.

As far as Jews were concerned, Polish dominant culture and Polish majority society followed their own antisemitic agendas—and it happened to accord with the German Nazi endeavor of the "Final Solution." Regarded as an opportunity or, in the eyes of the Catholic Church milieu as divine providence, this convergence is not the same as collaboration. Collaboration ceases with the absence of the invader, whereas Polish antisemitic aggression didn't stop with the defeat of the Third Reich and the end of WWII.

The Polish Context—After the War

Following the liberation by the Soviet and Polish armies in late fall 1944, the Alters stayed in Otwock, some twenty kilometers southeast of Warsaw. They resided at 2 Kochanowskiego Street[15] (today 6 Kochanowskiego Street) in the Szpinak Villa, next to the Jewish medical facilities, while waiting for the two armies to liberate Kutno. They then moved into their family house. Kutno was liberated on January 19, 1945. The Alters left Poland about a year and a half later. This was around the Kielce pogrom (July 1946) and a year after the pogroms in Rzeszów and Przemyśl (June 1945), as well as in Kraków (July 1945). In a conversation Terri depicted the departure of her family from Kutno as tumultuous and hurried, and that it was only possible because of the protection of some Soviet soldiers.

There is a historical record of an antisemitic murder in Kutno around that time. A soldier in the Polish army, Mordka Wertman, was shot dead on January 26, 1946. Unlike countless postwar murders of Jews by Poles, this one was neither anonymous nor secret. Wertman was killed in wartime fashion: in the open, in front of a large number of participating observers. His murderer was Jan Banasiak, a functionary in the Security Department (Urząd Bezpieczeństwa, UB), that was a terrain branch of the Ministry of Public Security.[16]

---

15 Cf. Jan Eljasz Alter-Kowalewski's membership card issued by the Warsaw-Białystok Medical Chamber in March 5, 1945.

16 Cf. Julian Kwiek, *Nie chcemy Żydów u siebie. Przejawy wrogości wobec Żydów w latach 1944–1947* ["We don't want Jews in our place."

The People's Republic of Poland was the first regime in Poland's history to extend Polish citizenship to Jews without being forced to do so by external powers. In addition to citizenship, it extended to Jews equal rights, both formally and in practice. As the regime lacked sociocultural legitimacy because of the widespread belief in the antisemitic myth of Judeo-communism, granting Jews equality under the law was viewed as proof of the myth. A thorough reeducation of society—if not a cultural revolution—was the only way out of that antisemitic vicious circle.

At the same time, however, in order to conform and benefit from the new system, the structures of power were joined by the masses including those who disapproved of the new state's principles and values. This is how Jan Banasiak could kill Mordka Wertman in Kutno; and this is how during the Kielce pogrom the functionaries of the regime could join the slaughterers of the same Jews they were supposed to protect. "We left Poland without even waiting for the Kielce pogrom," Terri said once.

Murders like the one in Kutno didn't occur in a social or cultural vacuum. They were preceded and more often than not followed by an antisemitic upheaval that may be called a pogrom atmosphere. It was clear that, despite the declared program and the actual intentions of the then elite, the new state was—at that point—unable to ensure security to Jews and whoever happened to be considered Jewish regardless of their own self-identification. Evoking Kielce while talking

Manifestations of hostility towards Jews in the years 1944–1947] (Warszawa: Wydawnictwo Nieoczywiste, 2021), 445.

about Kutno, as Terri did, is more than à propos. After some of the Kielce pogrom perpetrators were sentenced to death and executed, Polish workers went on strike in a gesture of solidarity with them. The authorities were frightened by the prospect of losing the meager legitimacy they had in the eyes of the social strata that was supposed to be their base. As a result, they abandoned the decree against antisemitism they were about to issue, distributed arms to Jewish committees, and opened the borders for Jewish emigration.

One hundred and fifty thousand Jews left Poland in 1946. Seventy thousand emigrated following the antisemitic tumult that occurred ten years later. The regime never reeducated society. Quite the opposite. Society "reeducated" the regime. In 1968, the authorities launched an antisemitic campaign that resulted in the exodus of fifteen thousand citizens, who were first humiliated by various administrative procedures and then stripped of Polish citizenship according to antisemitic criteria. Today, there are no more Jews than French living in Poland. This is why the conclusion of *My Kaddish: A Child Speaks from the Warsaw Ghetto*: "Poland has been cleansed."

The question of the Kutno murder was closed in court. Sentencing took place after the Kielce pogrom. The murderer of Mordka Wertman was acquitted. The court justified the judgment with the "argument" that Jan Banasiak acted "under the influence of strong excitement" (*działał pod wpływem silnego wzburzenia*).[17]

---

17 Ibid., 445.

Sixty years later

Sixty years later, Terri-Thérèse-Teresa-Klara decided to look back—to experience the terror lodged in her delicate body, the experience of which she had been running away from all her life. It also meant transgressing the commandments which the five-year-old Klara had learnt were punishable by death. She went to Golub-Dobrzyń, Kutno, and Warsaw. She went to the Umschlagplatz and the Treblinka fields of ashes.

I met her in 2004 during her first trip to Poland.[18] She didn't actually confront or consider the annihilation she so narrowly escaped. She engaged in the middle of it in full awareness that there was no possible comfort, no possible relief, no possibility of retrieving anything of any importance. Not even a possibility of mourning. After all, where could she mourn? Over the Warsaw parking lot under which Roza Ripin-Fuleder's profaned body lies mixed in with thousands of other profaned jumbled up bodies? Over the Treblinka concrete slabs poured out upon the remnants of nearly one million Jews, who were first tortured and murdered by the Germans, then reduced to ashes by the Germans, before being denuded again and violated by the Poles, as if making them available for all kinds of further abuse?[19]

---

18 Cf. Elżbieta Janicka, *Herbarium Polonorum (Heimatphotographie)*, *Studia Litteraria et Historica*, no. 9 (2020): 85–94, https://ispan.waw.pl/journals/index.php/slh/article/view/slh.2266/7049.

19 For instance, the mass murders of Jews by Poles of the summer of 1941— with the widely known live burnings in Jedwabne or Radziłów—are attributed to the Germans, and this in the very middle of the Treblinka fields of ashes. In the location of the former Treblinka train station, a monument was erected to a Pole who was among countless profiteers

She came because of the past. She also had to confront a present in which the past is not past. She was able to assess the extent to which nothing was reassessed, worked through, overcome. Not even the measurable—financial—aspect of the Holocaust of Poland's Jews. The fate of the Kutno family house and the respective estates of the Fuleders and the Alters are but three cases in point among countless others.

Her Kaddish

Terri was curious about what was initially supposed to be the Museum of the History of Polish Jews. There was a time when the endeavor instilled hope for a narrative that would put an end (once and for all) to the tried and tested antisemitic patterns: a narrative that would be faithful to knowledge and would be an act of historical justice, belated—but still. Then news about Polish state censorship got out, and at the last minute, in late fall 2014, the museum was renamed. The word POLIN—written in capital letters—was added to the initial appellation and entirely eclipsed it. Despite its apparently

---

swindling money, gold, and diamonds from Jews for a mouthful of water that sometimes was not even provided. Declared a rescuer of Jews by the local museum in 2011 (cf. Edward Kopówka and Paweł Rytel-Andrianik, *Polacy z okolic Treblinki ratujący Żydów* [Poles from the vicinity of Treblinka rescuing Jews,] [Oksford-Treblinka: Drohiczyńskie Towarzystwo Naukowe, Kuria Diecezjalna w Drohiczynie, 2011], 186–187), then by the Polish state in 2021 (cf. Jan Grabowski, "The New Wave of Holocaust Revisionism," *New York Times*, January 29, 2022, https://www.nytimes.com/2022/01/29/opinion/holocaust-poland-europe.html), the Pole in question was killed when the Germans or their helpers started shooting in order to make the Polish crowd retreat, as the train had to head for the nearby death camp.

neutral character ("Polin" in Hebrew means "Poland"), the term brought about one of the most toxic origin myths—the one about Jewish guests being generously received by Polish hosts. Invented in the late Middle Ages by the Christian majority, the Polin myth served throughout ages to legitimize inequality and domination/subordination as framing principles of Christian-Jewish relations. It also produced antisemitic exclusion and violence. Today, it precludes any rational conversation based on historical realities.

Terri was refused admission to the opening ceremony. "Brutal yet familiar," was her comment. This event is recounted in the preface to her memoir written by Simone Masson, Terri's daughter, who accompanied her on her journeys to Poland. In addition, somebody—a man—wanted to know if we hadn't turned up "by chance" for the discothèque taking place at the same time in the below ground part of the museum that was rented out for entertainment purposes.

We came back the following day. Terri couldn't resist commenting on the fact that the core exhibition was relegated to the basement. It was "As if it reminded me of something" (*Jakbym to już gdzieś widziała*). She had difficulty walking down the stairs, but declined to take the elevator. She held the handrail with her right hand and I was there on her left. Before our eyes, the known-by-heart, humiliating, boastful, and self-serving Polish narrative unfolded. I felt the blow hit her body.

After the deportations of 1942 and in expectation of further massacres, while knowing that they had nothing to expect from the "Aryan side," Jews dug bunkers all around the Warsaw Ghetto. They fought for survival and were murdered inside them after the ghetto had been set on fire by the

Germans during the Jewish uprising in April to May 1943. The bulk of the ghetto underground was never exhumed. Seventy years later, a part of this very underground was converted into an advertising space for the tale about Jewish guests mercifully received and generously hosted in the hospitable land of Polin—an instrument of emotional blackmail and a moral club used by Poles in reply to Jewish calls for equal rights over centuries. It seems that Walter Benjamin got it right: "not even the dead will be safe from the enemy, if he is victorious. And this enemy has not ceased to be victorious."[20]

Terri's first thought was to leave the exhibition immediately. After a while, however, she went deeper into the underground and started a kaddish—her kaddish—a laic version of what once used to be a prayer. She did it clearly in a gesture of denouncing the defilement of the place. Rather than a way of bidding farewell, it was her way of reconnecting and standing in solidarity with those she had to cut herself off from in order to survive. It was also an act of reconnecting with herself. This is *My Kaddish: A Child Speaks from the Warsaw Ghetto*, her book.

Towards the end of her testimony, Terri-Thérèse-Teresa-Klara confesses to the powerful impulse she had to run through Warsaw crying out the horror of "the murder of Jews that was a success," to amplify what she describes as "the dying lament of that world that was to be my world." Now that she is no more, her words remain and resonate among other words

---

20 Walter Benjamin, *On the Concept of History* (1940), trans. Dennis Redmond, Marxists.org, accessed 31 May 2023, https://www.marxists.org/reference/archive/benjamin/1940/history.htm.

full of fury and despair. As from this line of Job engraved at the Warsaw Umschlagplatz: "O, earth, cover not thou my blood, and let my cry have no resting-place." And as another little girl from the Warsaw Ghetto put it in her recollection from then and there: "because death is the final rest / because death is eternal rage."[21]

Elżbieta Janicka
Warsaw, spring 2023

21 Irena Klepfisz, "Bashert" (1982), Madison Public Library, accessed July 18, 2023, https://www.madisonpubliclibrary.org/engagement/poetry/poem-a-day/bashert.

Recollections of Terri

I met Terri in 1970, in Toronto, Canada. I had just accepted my first job, as an assistant professor of Sanskrit at the University of Toronto. Terri was a successful producer-director at the Canadian Broadcasting Company and we met because she intended to do a program about ancient India in which I had a part. The program was not made, but we ended up getting married.

At the time, I was preoccupied with the Holocaust. This drew me to Terri because I knew she had lived as a child in the Warsaw Ghetto (having been born in Golub-Dobrzyń in 1937). I assumed we would spend hours every day talking about the Holocaust. I was wrong. Terri would not, or could not, talk about it. I respected her need to avoid the topic since she was so willing to talk incisively about other important matters—we never lacked for deep conversation. She was ferociously intelligent and had a moral compass to match her intellect, as well as a remarkable talent for empathy. Suffering of any kind distressed her.

I assumed that Terri chose (if it was even a choice) not to speak about the Holocaust because she had suffered too much. This is true. But what I did not understand for a very long time was that this suffering was not in the past tense. She was still suffering in the present. Not in the obvious way of "Ach, woe is me," but in the more subtle manner of feeling compelled to "act out" (her words) certain situations over and over. As she told me, and as she explains in this book, she was like a living testimony to Freud's repetition compulsion, that is, the need to repeat situations in the hope of achieving better outcomes. I was a fascinated and also deeply saddened bystander to her efforts.

It is not entirely true that Terri would never talk about her life in the Ghetto. A few times she did tell me what happened. It was mesmerizing and heartbreaking at the same time. It affected me deeply to hear this story. I suppose I did not give sufficient note to how it made her feel and what consequences trauma of this kind can have in later life.

Another thing that attracted us to one another was that we were both deeply connected to psychoanalysis. While I was in Poone, India, I read the three volume biography of Sigmund Freud by Ernest Jones and determined that I wanted to become a psychoanalyst. So, while teaching Sanskrit I also applied to the Psychoanalytic Institute in Toronto and was accepted for training. It would last for nearly ten years, as is standard. Terri was in analysis when I met her, in an attempt to better understand her early childhood. Alas, it was not to be. I remember clearly how frustrated she was—I, myself, reacted with anger—when her analyst, whom she assumed was Jewish (he was not; in fact, he was quite the opposite), "interpreted" her continual reference to the "Aryan side" when describing Warsaw and the Warsaw Ghetto as a compulsion to divide the world into good and bad. Why should one not talk of sides? He was so ignorant about the Holocaust that he did not even understand that she was simply making a geographical point, not an ethical one.

This alarming incident became, for me, the beginning of my skepticism concerning my new profession. For if somebody could be so wrong on such an important issue, who was to know if they could not be equally wrong on other issues as well? It felt to me like a dangerous undertaking, attempting to understand the life trajectory of another person. You could quickly come up against the limits of your own understanding, or your historical knowledge, or your empathy, or your political convictions, your class, your gender, your privileges, even your language, your religion, your ethnicity. The barriers, it struck me, were insurmountable.

I began, even as I was undertaking my training as a Freudian analyst, to develop an increasing skepticism toward the very idea of analysis, indeed, of therapy in general. (Later I was to embody these doubts in three books: *The Assault on Truth*; *Final Analysis*; and *Against Therapy*). Terri shared some of my skepticism, but she retained a far greater belief in the power of psychoanalysis to understand the past than I did. This can be seen in the book in your hands. She attempts, far more successfully than I would have thought possible, to translate psychoanalytic ideas into explanations for her own behavior post-Holocaust. She has made sense of her suffering.

It is not for me to decide whether she is right or wrong, but I must say that the very attempt itself is, possibly, unique. I read a lot of Holocaust literature (and have been doing so since I was fifteen), but I have yet to see a psychological portrait of the Warsaw Ghetto by a former resident as compelling as Terri's. It is, in my estimation, an extraordinary achievement, one that should be welcome to all people interested in the Holocaust.

Yes, Terri was deeply damaged by her years in the Warsaw Ghetto as a child. But she was able to do something exceptional: understand that damage in psychological terms. As I have said, she was a remarkable human being. I feel honored to have known Terri, to have been married to her, to have been the recipient of her deep wisdom and, in later life, her friendship.

After we separated, Terri became increasingly interested in living a more Jewish life. I am Jewish, but neither of us were religious and we did not bring Simone up in any religious fashion, to the point of not observing Jewish holidays. I understand that she felt the need to get closer to her roots, to the Jewish people. She went so far as to return to Warsaw, searching (mostly in vain) for remnants of her prewar life.

The older she got, the closer she came to reflecting on her experience in the Holocaust. (She had never stopped reading: we were both great admirers of Primo Levi, and not great fans of Hannah Arendt's *Eichmann in Jerusalem*, which we read together and whose thesis about "the banality of evil" we rejected together). This is how she came to write *My Kaddish*. The tragedy is that had she done so earlier in her life, she might not only have made sense of her suffering, but could possibly have prevented the distorted repetitions of the trauma she suffered in her childhood into her adulthood.

What I saw is that Terri needed to live on the edge: she found it exhilarating to put herself into dangerous situations, where the outcome was unclear at best. Gambling was one example. She liked to "escape" situations that seemed hopeless. She had done so once and seemed doomed to go on repeating the close encounters with death or near-death, much of her adult life. No doubt, nothing in life prepares anyone for what Terri experienced in the Warsaw Ghetto, so one cannot possibly know how people will react.

After the war, her father wanted to continue to practice medicine in Poland. But when he and Terri's mother witnessed the virulent antisemitism that had still not disappeared, they chose to go to Paris instead. Terri was delighted:

she was precocious, and within months was speaking fluent French and doing exceedingly well in school. She loved Paris. At nine she was sitting in cafes (alas, smoking!) and arguing about existentialism. The French found her brilliant and delightful. She was both. One can only wonder what sort of life she would have had in Paris. But the French would not allow her father to practice medicine, the love of his life, and soon he accepted a post in a small bleak town in the Canadian West. Terri ceased to flourish socially (antisemitism was also alive and well in Canada—she told me she remembered signs in parks saying no dogs or Jews allowed).

Terri had many remarkable gifts. She also had insurmountable flaws. The combination of these created a volatile mixture which seemed to fuel the repeated moves from one professional pursuit to the next. Her gifts included the ability to swiftly assimilate masses of new information, an exquisite intellect, a drive against complacency, awareness and genuine concern for the feelings of others, and a total abhorrence of injustice of any kind. I believe that her two major flaws were her undoing—the urge to run from her past (really at any cost to herself) and the urge to self-sabotage. No doubt both were dark remnants of her past, lodged deeply inside her psyche. She was finally able to overcome these to some degree, but not until her final years.

Though we divorced in 1982, we remained close friends until her death in 2016. She was a good friend to me—a beacon of wisdom, insight, empathy, and generosity. Despite the weight of her past, she always managed to bring lightness and joy to whatever she was doing, whether it was sipping an espresso at 11:00 p.m., or working on a legal contract at

2:00 a.m. Even more amazing was the generosity that marked her every interaction. She was never stingy with her time or energy. She was up for anything, especially if it involved taking a big risk or indulging in a small pleasure. This world is poorer because Terri is no longer in it.

Jeffrey Moussaieff Masson
Sydney
July 30, 2018.

About the Author

Terri Masson, born Klara Alter, enriched the lives of all who knew her. She was a free-spirited, incredibly generous, and loving person. Possessed with creativity, a fierce intellect, and a sense of justice and possibility, she built many careers over her lifetime: journalist, television producer, philosophy instructor, taxi driver, lawyer, business consultant, and, in the last years of her life, tireless advocate for homeowners fighting foreclosures by the big banks. Throughout her life, Terri forged deep relationships, including with her many friends, with her husband and then good friend Jeff, with her partner of thirty-four years, Deborah, and with her daughter, Simone.

Index

Printed in the USA
CPSIA information can be obtained
at www.ICGtesting.com
JSHW081514040324
58548JS00007B/261